CANADA*

BRITAIN*

UNITED STATES OF AMERICA

MALTA

7

Dependencies, colonies and protectorates of U.K., Australia or New Zealand

BAHAMAS 1973

22

③ JAMAICA 1962

⑩

24

GRENADA 1974

BARBADOS 1966

TRINIDAD & TOBAGO 1962

GAMBIA 1965

SIERRA LEONE 1960

GHANA 1957

NIGER

GUYANA 1966

2

① Ascension I.
② Bermuda
③ British Honduras
④ British Solomon Is.
⑤ Cook I.
⑥ Falkland Is.
⑦ Gibraltar
⑧ Gilbert and Ellice Is.
⑨ Hong Kong
⑩ Leeward Is.
⑪ Macquairie Is.
⑫ New Britain
⑬ New Guinea
⑭ New Hebrides
⑮ New Ireland
⑯ Papua
⑰ Rhodesia
⑱ St Helena
⑲ Seychelles
⑳ South Georgia
㉑ South Sandwich
㉒ Turks and Caicos Is.
㉓ Tristan da Cunha
㉔ Windward Is.

①

18

23

6

20

21

CYPRUS 1960

PAKISTAN 1947
(LEFT COMMONWEALTH 1972)

INDIA 1947

EAST PAKISTAN
(BANGLADESH FROM 1972)

⑨

DA 1962

KENYA 1963

NIA 1964

MALAWI 1964

1964

CEYLON 1948
(NOW SRI LANKA)

MALAYSIA 1963

SINGAPORE 1961

⑲

⑧

⑮

⑬

⑫

NAURU 1968

⑧

⑯

④

MAURITIUS 1968

WESTERN SAMOA 1970

ANA 1966

SWAZILAND 1968

OTHO 1966

⑭

FIJI 1970

⑤

AUSTRALIA*

TONGA 1970

he Commonwealth and
he United States, circa 1970

NEW ZEALAND*

The Commonwealth, circa 1970   *Founder members   Dates refer to dates of accession

First published 1974
Macdonald & Co (Publishers) Limited
Macdonald Educational
London W1A 2LG
© 1974 Macdonald & Co
(Publishers) Limited

Printed in England by
Hazell Watson & Viney Ltd
Aylesbury, Bucks

Edited by Tim Healey
Research: Bridget Hadaway

ISBN 0 356 04454 8
Library of Congress Catalog Card
No. 77-172434

*F
914.203
U59
V. 8*

We wish to thank the following individuals and organizations for their assistance and for making available material in their Collections.

Associated Newspapers *page 65(TR)*
Associated Press *pages 46(R), 47(BR)*
Australian News and Information Bureau *pages 66, 67(L) (CR) (BR)*
Barnaby's Picture Library *pages 56, 60–61*
Barratt's Photo Press *page 57(B)*
Batchelor, John *cover (T), pages 16(R), 36, 37(T), 48(BL), 50(T) (B)*
Berliner Illustrierte *page 9(BR)*
Bettman Archive *page 26(L)*
B.I.P.P.A. *page 63(BR)*
Bolt, Anne *page 79(BL)*
British Aircraft Corporation *page 51(B)*
Camera Press *cover (BR), pages 28(TR), 35(BL), 40(R), 45(BL), 59(TR), 73*
    Colman Doyle *page 65(BR)*
    Stephen Goldblatt *page 33(BR)*
    Regina Hamilton *page 85(BR)*
    David Moore *page 82(BL)*
    N.A.S.A. *page 83(TC)*
    William Vandivert *page 31(B)*
Cavendish Laboratory, University of Cambridge *page 34(B)*
Central Office of Information *page 71(TL)*
Central Press *pages 24(R), 64*
Chicago Tribune *page 85(TL)*
Communist Party Library *page 13(BR)*
Conservative Research Department *page 77(BR)*
Crown copyright *page 30(L)*
Culver Pictures Incorporated *cover (L), page 75*
Cynwyd Investments *page 72(BL)*
Daily Telegraph Magazine *page 71(TR)*

Dallas Notes *page 43(BR)*
Der Spiegel *page 62*
Domenica del Corriere, Milan: G.B. Bertelli *page 49(B)*
Earl Beatty *page 8*
Electricity Council *pages 54(L) (R), 55(T)*
E.M.I. Electronics Limited *page 35(R)*
Fleischer *page 57(TL)*
Fox Photos *pages 17(TR), 78(BR)*
General Motors *page 41(B)*
George Orwell Archive *page 81(CR)*
Gernsheim *pages 25(TL), 74(R)*
G.L.C. Photographic Library *page 4(L)*
Hulton Picture Library *title page (BC) 11(B), 12(L), 14(R), 22(BL), 30(R), 53(TL), 56(TL), 76(L), 79(TR), 81(CL)*
Huntingdon Hartford *cover (BC)*
Imperial War Museum *pages 7(T), 9(TL), 18(R), 22(R), 25(TC)*
Institute of Social History, Amsterdam *page 11(TL)*
Instituto Geografico de Agostini S.P.A. Novara *pages 27(C), 41(T)*
Keystone Press *pages 19(BR), 59(TL), 60(T), 69(B), 74(C)*
King Features *page 32(R)*
Kunstgeweber Museum, Zurich *page 57(TR)*
Labour Party *page 77(TR)*
Library of Congress *pages 25(TR), 44(R)*
    Dorothy Lange *page 25(BL)*
L'Illustration *page 12(R)*
L.S.E. *page 5(TR)*
Lords Gallery *page 27(CL)*
Magnum Photos: Marc Riboud *page 77(TL)*
    Burke Uzzle *page 43(BL)*
Mansell Collection *pages 5(TC), 70(L), 72(R)*
Mary Evans Picture Library *page 5(BR)*
Mayne Roger *pages 44(L), 45(BR), 63(TC) (TR), 72(TL)*
Metropolitan Museum of Art: Alfred Steigetz collection *page 80*
Motif Editions *page 81(TR)*
Mount Palomar Observatory *page 82(R)*
Musee des Arts Decoratifs, Paris *pages 4–5*
N.A.S.A. *title page (BR), pages 53(TR), 83(TR) (BC) (BR)*
National Archives *page 42(TL)*
National Films Archive: Roger Manvell *page 29(CR)*
National Gallery of Canada, Ottawa *page 69(T)*
New Yorker Magazine Incorporated, 1965 *page 35(CL)*
New Zealand House *page 67(T)*
Nichols, Harvey *page 79(TL)*
Odhams *page 56(BL)*

Omnibus Society Collection *page 26(L) (R)*
Paul Popper *pages 22(TL), 23(TR), 33(BL), 40(L), 51(TR), 55(R), 81(B)*
Pesticides and Pollution by Kenneth Melanby, Collins 1969 *page 85(CR)*
Picturepoint *page 48(TR)*
Playboy Magazine *page 25(BR)*
Rex Features *pages 55(B), 63(BL)*
Rosner and Sons *title page (TR)*
Royal Astrological Society *page 82(TL)*
Science Museum, London *page 37(BR)*
S.C.R. Photographic Library *pages 9(TR), 10*
Sheldon Swope Art Gallery, Indiana *pages 52–53*
Snark: Le Petit Journal *page 5(TL)*
Sphere *page 51(TL)*
Sudd-Verlag, Munich *pages 6(R), 13(L)*
Swayne, Eric *page 79(BL)*
Taslemka: Elegante Welt *page 24(L)*
Time Incorporated: Life *page 43(T)*
Time Magazine *page 42(R)*
Transworld Features Syndicate *pages 45(TR), 63(TL), 65(BL)*
U.K. Atomic Energy Authority *page 39*
Ullstein *page 78(L)*
United Artists *page 29(BR)*
United Press International *pages 13(BR), 42(BL), 45(TL)*
U.S.A.F. *page 37(BL)*
U.S. Army Department *title page (BL), pages 19(BL), 21(BR)*
U.S. Department of the Interior, Washington *page 46(L)*
U.S. Navy Department *page 18(L)*
U.S.P.G. *page 58(R)*
Victoria and Albert Museum *page 32(L)*
Viollet *page 33(T)*
Vogue *page 78(CR)*
Walt Disney productions, Caligari Archive *page 29(BL)*
Warner Brothers *page 79(TC)*
World Health Organization, Geneva *page 71(BL)*
Yale University Library *page 81(TL)*

Cover: (L) Propaganda for women's suffrage before World War One.
(TR) Buick car, 1949.
(BC) American recruitment poster of World War One.
(BR) Saturn V blasts off.
Title page (opposite): (TL) Film magazine cover, between the wars.
(BL) Churchill and Roosevelt.
(TC) Cigarette card shows how to fit on a gas-mask, World War Two.
(BC) Fashions at Ascot in the 1920's.
(TR) The "New Look" of the 1940's
(BR) The moon landing, 1969.

Macdonald
Educational

R J Unstead

Incredible Century

A Pictorial History
1901-1970

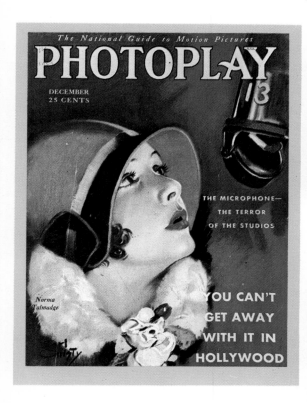

Volume Eight

Our century has been, in every sense, incredible. When it began, Britain ruled a world-wide empire and the United States played little part in international affairs. No man had flown in a powered aircraft or listened to a radio; few had ridden in a motor car or seen a moving picture. Medical skill was so rudimentary that the removal of an appendix was a very dangerous undertaking. The vast majority of people were poor, insecure and dominated by the ruling classes.

Since 1900, our world has been transformed at a fantastic pace. Less than 70 years after the Wright brothers' brief flight, man has landed on the moon. Cinema, which had been the marvel of the world at the turn of the century, has already seen the passing of its golden age. Intensive production has made food, clothes and manufactured goods available on a mass scale, so that most people are better off than ever before. Yet we live in an age of violence; two world wars have involved whole populations at a terrible cost. The wars have brought about the decline of Britain and the rise of America as the most important influence in the English-speaking world.

Macdonald Educational

R J Unstead

Incredible Century

On the left, the Earth as it was seen from the Moon in 1969. In that year, scientists achieved the incredible feat of landing two American astronauts on the Moon's surface. Man has reached beyond his own planet and is poised for new discoveries in space.

In this last book of a series of eight, we have tried to draw a picture of the English-speaking world during the first 70 years of the century. We have outlined the principal events, ideas and social changes that have occurred and that have culminated in the remarkable achievement of the lunar landing.

In some ways, the picture is a disturbing one, but change is usually a disturbing process. Many of the great achievements of the century—motoring, aviation, nuclear fission, pesticides and mass production, for example, have brought new problems. Yet there is plenty of evidence to suggest that man has the ability to solve them.

Contents

The First Years

In 1900, Europe stood at the peak of her power. The energy, inventiveness and aggression of her peoples had given her dominance over practically all the world, except the United States and Japan. Although large parts of Europe remained backward, her output of manufactured goods accounted for two-thirds of the world's exports.

Europe's capitals, Paris, London, Rome, Vienna, Berlin, were the cultural centres of the world. Yet European society was disfigured by gross inequality between rich and poor. Some of the workers were beginning to organize and the early years of the century saw frequent strikes and protests. Only in Russia, however, was there any serious fear of revolution. The threat of military force was an accepted part of international politics. All European governments were arming themselves and negotiating alliances and diplomatic understandings. Many already felt that a great war between the European powers was inevitable. Alliances were felt to be a necessary precaution—yet they created an atmosphere of mistrust that made war all the more likely.

Poverty in London, a back street in Stepney, 1909. In his massive survey (1903), Charles Booth estimated that almost a third of London's population was poor and eight to nine per cent was near starvation.

Right: the elegance of wealth in Paris. The city drew writers, artists and musicians, as well as wealthy pleasure-seekers, from all over the English-speaking world.

The two decades before 1914 saw the final flowering of an era of privilege. In later years, the upper classes looked back on this as a vanished golden age. To the poor it was a time of suffering and want.

Violence in America, a portent of the future; the murder of President McKinley in 1901 by an anarchist. Anarchists caused alarm throughout Europe and America with their bomb attacks and assassinations.

Edward VII, Britain's jovial monarch. His visit to Paris in 1903 did much to restore friendly relations with France at a time when Britain was becoming nervous about Germany's increasing power.

Europe's monarchs were mostly related to each other through Queen Victoria. They still played influential parts in politics.

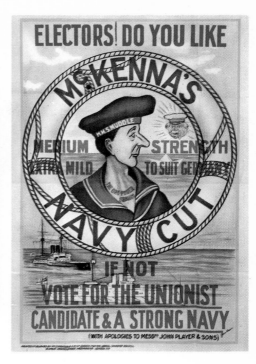

ELECTORS! DO YOU LIKE McKENNA'S NAVY CUT
MEDIUM STRENGTH
EXTRA MILD TO SUIT GERMANY
IF NOT VOTE FOR THE UNIONIST CANDIDATE & A STRONG NAVY
(WITH APOLOGIES TO MESS"* JOHN PLAYER & SONS)

Poster of 1908 attacks McKenna, the Liberal First Lord of the Admiralty. He was alleged to be skimping on building dreadnoughts, a type of super-battleship. Germany's naval programme threatened Britain's supremacy at sea.

What lay ahead?

In 1900, a man who was familiar with the remarkable science-fiction of Jules Verne and H. G. Wells might have predicted the moon landing.

If he was well-informed, he would have heard of Marconi's wireless signals and of attempts to build a flying machine.

He would certainly have known about motor cars, telephones, moving pictures, department stores, electric trains, traffic jams and huge sprawling cities. All of these were already in existence.

What he could hardly have foreseen was the speed with which these inventions and developments would dominate society all over the world. And it is practically certain that he would not have envisaged the decline of Europe's domination of the globe, or the havoc caused by two world wars.

Jules Verne's space shell from *A Journey to the Moon* (1865). Science fiction writers foresaw some of the inventions that have made this century incredible.

World War One:
the trenches

Was the war that broke out in 1914 an inevitable conflict? Certainly, Germany's ambition to become a world power could only be realized through war. For more than twenty years, her aggressive stance, her military and naval programmes, had kept Europe in a state of tension. A network of alliances was formed—the Triple Alliance of Germany, Austria and Italy; the Dual Alliance of France and Russia; the "understanding" between Britain and France. Russia championed the Slav peoples in the Balkans. This situation was made all the more dangerous by imperial rivalries, ardent patriotism and a readiness to accept war as the means of solving problems. Any incident, any affront to national pride, could bring about an explosion. The incident occurred at Sarajevo, where an archduke's assassination led directly to the most destructive war that the world had so far known.

It was to be a war that baffled the generals. It was a war of deadlock, with immense armies hidden from each other in trenches, a war of mass slaughter and of civilian participation to an extent never known before.

Austrian stamp commemorating the assassination of Archduke Franz Ferdinand and his wife.

The Murder at Sarajevo

On 28 June 1914, in the Balkan town of Sarajevo, a student named Gavrilo Princip fired two shots into a royal car. Archduke Franz Ferdinand, heir to the Austro-Hungarian Empire, and his wife, died almost immediately.

The assassination plot had been hatched in Serbia and the conspirators were aided by the Black Hand, a Serbian secret society. Austria, backed by Germany, sent Serbia some harsh demands. Although Serbia accepted all except one, Austria declared war on 28 July.

Russia, friend of the Slavs, mobilized her armies. Austria's ally, Germany, then declared war. Since France was bound to support Russia, Germany attacked France by advancing through Belgium. This invasion of a neutral country made the British decide to fight. On 4 August 1914, Britain and Germany were at war.

Kindly gesture in the midst of war: a German soldier lights a cigarette for his prisoner.

Generally speaking, soldiers did not share the civilians' hatred of the enemy. They saw themselves as fellow-victims of a gigantic muddle, forced into hopeless attacks planned by generals who seemed unaware of conditions at the front.

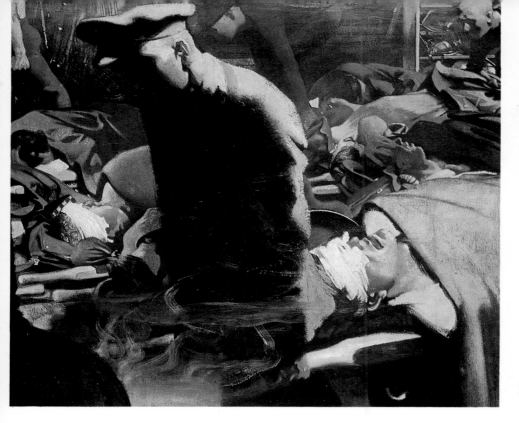

Left: *Gassed and Wounded*, a painting by Eric Kennington.

The poet, Wilfred Owen, described the horror of trench warfare, with the mud and rain "guttering down in waterfalls of slime", the shelling that filled the "shrieking air" and poison gas which brought "blood come gargling from the froth-corrupted lungs".

Below: the German offensive of 1914. According to the Schlieffen Plan, two German armies would sweep across Belgium to encircle Paris, while other armies pinned down French strength around Verdun.

The offensive failed only because of British resistance at Mons and stubborn French defence organized by General Joffre. When the Germans veered south-east, he counter-attacked and drove them back across the Marne. After this, the opposing armies dug in. The stalemate of trench warfare was to last for four years.

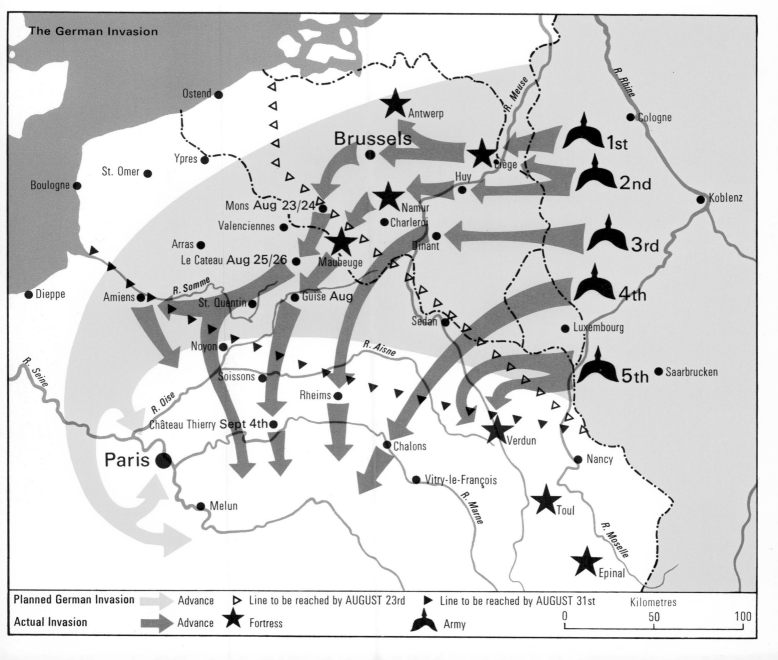

The German Invasion

Planned German Invasion — Advance — ▷ Line to be reached by AUGUST 23rd — ► Line to be reached by AUGUST 31st

Actual Invasion — Advance — ★ Fortress — Army

Kilometres
0   50   100

World War One: Germany defeated

While the generals tried to break the stalemate of trench warfare in the west by launching gigantic offensives, the Russians suffered huge losses in holding the enemy on the Eastern Front. 1915 saw the Allies' vain effort to knock out Turkey at Gallipoli and, as the war proceeded, further subordinate campaigns took place in East Africa, in the Middle East and northern Italy. At sea, after one inconclusive engagement at Jutland, each side concentrated on trying to starve the other—the Allies by blockade, the Germans by submarine attacks on merchant shipping.

Then came the Russian collapse of 1917. This enabled the Germans to switch reinforcements to the west for the great offensive of March 1918. It almost succeeded and was only halted because of German exhaustion and the timely arrival of fresh American troops. The Allies counter-attacked and, with dramatic suddenness, Germany broke. Her armies were not totally defeated but, behind them, civilians rioted, the fleet mutinied and the Kaiser fled to Holland. On 11 November 1918, an armistice brought the war to its end.

Admiral Beatty's battle-cruisers in action at Jutland, June 1916.

War at sea

The German naval policy was to keep their fleet behind minefields while surface raiders and submarines attacked merchant ships. Surface raiders were soon eliminated, but the U-boat campaign almost brought Britain to her knees.

In 1916, the German Grand Fleet had the better of the sharp engagement at Jutland. However, as Jellicoe's main fleet came racing to the rescue, the Germans retired to the safety of their minefields. They never ventured out again until their surrender in 1918.

Lenin in a German train on his way to Petrograd to lead the revolution.

Revolution in Russia

In March 1917, the Russian Revolution began in Petrograd, when a garrison revolt spread like wildfire. The Tsar abdicated and a Socialist government under Kerensky tried to carry on the war.

In November, the Bolshevik leader, Lenin, emerged from hiding to overthrow Kerensky and end the war. He accepted harsh terms for Russia at the Treaty of Brest-Litovsk.

Thus, Germany was free to transfer troops to the west in a final bid for victory. It resulted, in fact, in Germany's defeat.

An American Balloon Company on the Western Front. After two and a half years of neutrality, the U.S. entered the war because of the German submarine campaign. It also became known that Germany was urging Mexico to attack America.

General Pershing reached France with the first American division in 1917, but it took time to train civilians. Until 1918, the numbers involved in actual fighting were small.

But the knowledge that American manpower and production had come in on the Allied side had an enormous effect on morale.

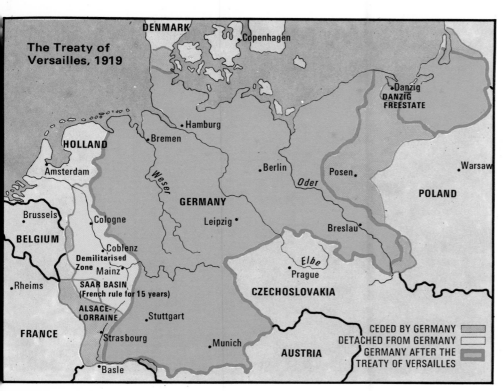

Left and above: Germany after the Treaty of Versailles and the Kaiser who abdicated in 1918. The Treaty was bitterly resented by the Germans. Their feelings of grievance were a cause of World War Two.

9

The Workers Organize

When the century opened, working-class standards of living were rarely much above the poverty line. Wages were low and hours long. Benefits such as unemployment pay, sick pay and old age pensions hardly existed. However, in Britain, workers like the dockers had shown that they could unite to win better terms of employment. The trade union movement had created the Labour Party to represent workers in Parliament. Progress was turbulent; strikes were often accompanied by violence, especially in America, and it was widely believed that a war would produce revolution. Yet, although the Communist International was formed in Russia to spread world-wide revolution, Britain and the U.S. retained their traditional forms of parliamentary government.

Fear of Communism agitated the ruling classes in Britain and America during and after the inter-war years, but the revolution never came. Most workers wanted, not Communism, but better conditions and higher wages. They supported their trade unions and, in Britain, the Labour Party. They acted through peaceful negotiation.

Communism and the West

The Russian Revolution and the actions of the Bolsheviks (the leading party of the Russian revolutionaries) alarmed the victorious Allies. The Bolsheviks had withdrawn from World War One, refused to pay foreign debts, confiscated property. They had overthrown the aristocracy and avowed their intention of organizing revolution throughout the world.

Russia was not invited to the Peace Conference and a cordon of new states was created to keep Communism away from the West.

After Lenin's death in 1924, Stalin, his successor, realized that hopes of world revolution were misplaced. He decided to concentrate upon his own country. However, the Communist parties elsewhere were not entirely abandoned. They still drew inspiration from Moscow; members paid visits to Russia and often aroused alarm that was probably out of all proportion to their importance.

"Red scares" occurred from time to time in Britain and America. In the 1950's, for example, the American Senator McCarthy conducted a "witch-hunt", denouncing figures in all walks of public life as secret Communists.

The public steadfastly refused to vote Communist. The party therefore turned its attention to the trade unions, in which, at least in Britain, it has secured some dominance.

Symbol of victorious revolution: a Russian Red Guard stands by the Tsar's empty throne. Abroad, people wondered, "Could it happen here?"

WE WANT EVOLUTION NOT REVOLUTION — VOTE LABOUR

The British Labour Party

In 1906, Britain's Labour Party won 29 seats in Parliament and one of its M.P.'s, an ex-docker, entered the Liberal Cabinet. The party supported World War One and showed such respectable moderation that it actually took office in 1924. Ramsay MacDonald became the first Labour Prime Minister.

Lacking an overall majority, he was unable to introduce many reforms and was defeated when it was suggested that the Labour Party had connections with Communist Russia. The failure of the 1926 General Strike hurt the Labour Party's image but MacDonald was back in office in 1929. He was expelled from the party for agreeing to form a National Government with the other parties in 1931.

For the next 14 years, Labour had only a handful of M.P.'s, held together by the moderation and skill of Clement Attlee. 1945 brought an overwhelming victory. Attlee and his colleagues were able to bring about a social revolution. Britain's basic industries were nationalized and the National Health Service was created.

Labour lost the 1951 Election and remained in opposition until the narrow victory of 1964, which was repeated more comfortably in 1966. Harold Wilson took office promising growth and social reform.

Left: 1923 Election poster stresses that British Socialism means gradual reform, not revolution. Labour's record has proved the point.

Below: General Strike, 1926, an armoured car protects a food convoy. The strike lasted nine days. It collapsed without much violence.

Between the Wars

Throughout the 1920's, Europe struggled with the problems of recovering from the effects of World War One. Unemployment and poverty were widespread, especially in Germany and Austria. By 1929, there were signs of better times ahead. Production was rising, trade had improved and international ill-feeling seemed to have simmered down. The great popular innovations—radio, motoring, cinema, contributed to a general feeling of well-being. Suddenly, in October 1929, a massive economic crash occurred in America.

America's importance in trade and finance was now so great, that when Americans lost confidence in their economy, the effects spread all over the world. The great Depression of the 1930's brought disaster to millions. There were six million unemployed in Germany. In despair, the German people turned to Hitler and the Nazis came to power in 1933. Italy was already in Mussolini's grip and, in Spain, Franco's revolt led to the tragedy of the Spanish Civil War. Fascist parties were founded in Britain, France and America, but in these countries democracy survived without undue strain.

The despair of unemployment, bane of the inter-war years. In Britain, after a brief post-war boom, unemployment rose to a million in 1920. It did not fall below this figure for the next 20 years.

In 1931, nearly three million workers were unemployed and living on the dole. It was not enough to keep them and their families healthy.

Right: saloon of a luxury liner. Notice the backless evening gowns, considered very daring at the time.

This was the era when the "Bright Young Things" found a new freedom to enjoy themselves. Goods were cheap and prices stable. Those with money could have a good time.

Roosevelt's New Deal

The picture above shows Franklin D. Roosevelt meeting a farm worker during his 1932 Presidential campaign.

The Great Depression produced mass unemployment, poverty and under-production in America. Roosevelt was elected on his promise to introduce a "New Deal". This would reform banking, improve unemployment relief and provide a vast programme of public works.

The New Deal worked. Unemployment fell (though it was not cured), business, industry and farming were set on the road to recovery. Roosevelt had restored American confidence.

Inflation (when money loses its value) in Germany after World War One. These women have exchanged their family silver for the farmer's sack of flour. People resorted to bartering. Fear of renewed inflation helped to bring Hitler to power. Democracy seemed to have failed.

British anti-Fascist poster of the 1930's. Oswald Mosley's British Union of Fascists provoked violence and anti-Semitism in London

The British Empire

When World War One broke out, many people expected the British Empire to break up, but the reverse happened. The Dominions (Canada, Australia, New Zealand and South Africa) put a million men into the field. At the Peace Conference, they and India were represented separately. Moreover, all were accepted as full members of the League of Nations.

Although the Dominions were self-governing nations, they did not, however, have full control of their external affairs. Then, in 1931, the Statute of Westminster confirmed the Balfour Report of 1926 which said that they were "autonomous communities . . . equal in status". The British Commonwealth had come into being.

At this stage, it was only a "white man's club". It did not include the races of Africa and Asia who made up the majority of subjects under British rule. The most important of these were the people of India. Britain was granting self-government, but not fast enough to satisfy the Indian nationalists. The years between the wars were troubled.

A brilliant barrister, M. K. Gandhi, led a campaign of "civil disobedience"—a policy of refusing to co-operate with the British authorities. Gandhi himself insisted that the campaign be waged peacefully, but acts of violence were committed by both sides. At Amritsar, for example, the British General Dyer ordered his troops to fire on an illegally assembled crowd. 379 Indians were killed.

King George V on his yacht. He became head of the Commonwealth in 1926.

Right: Mohandas Gandhi on his way to attend the Round Table Conference in London, 1931, when discussions took place on India becoming a Dominion.

Gandhi was both saint and politician, organizer of civil disobedience and thorn in the side of the British (who put him in prison). He was, nevertheless, a supporter of the Commonwealth and he curbed his extreme followers.

The British Empire at its height in
1935, between the wars.
   The map shows the Dominions
(self-governing), the colonies
(administered by British officials)
and mandates (ex-enemy territories,
like Palestine, Tanganyika and
Togoland. They were entrusted to

Britain by the League of Nations until
ready for self-rule).
   Notice the migration figures; far
more people left Britain to settle in
the Empire than left the Empire to
come to Britain. You can also see
how·trade fell during the worst
Depression years (1930–36).

Migration between Great Britain and the British Empire

To the Empire from Great Britain

1925-29

Average annual migration
Figures in thousands

Australia 35

1930

Canada 52

New Zealand 8
South Africa 3

Rest of British Empire 17
excluding Irish Free State

(Other countries 33)

to

total 148

To Great Britain from the Empire

1925-29   1930

Australia 8
New Zealand 1
South Africa 1

Canada and rest of
British Empire 32
excluding Irish Free State

(Other countries 13)

total 55

to

Trade between Great Britain and the British Empire

Figures in £millions

1925   1930   1935   1938

Ottawa Conference, 1932

Map

NEW
ZEALAND

AUSTRALIA

Tonga   •Fiji
     Solomon Is
     •Ellice Is   NEW
               GUINEA
          Administered by Australia

BORNEO   •Christmas I.

Hong
Kong   MALAYA

          •Cocos Is

     • Andaman Is

BU

          ◌ Ceylon

Pitcairn I.

Newfoundland
dominion,
reverted
to crown
colony, 1933

CANADA

GREAT
BRITAIN

          ⁂ Maldive Is

BRITISH
HONDURAS   • Bermuda
          Bahama Is
          Malta Cyprus   PALESTINE
Jamaica Gibraltar   Aden
     • Leeward Is
     • Windward Is   Anglo-Egyptian   SOMALILAND
     • Barbados   mandate   UGANDA
     • Trinidad   KENYA
BRITISH   CAMEROONS SUDAN   TANGANYIKA • Seychelle Is
GUIANA   TOGOLAND
     GAMBIA   • Zanzibar
     SIERRA   • Aldabra Is
     LEONE   GOLD COAST
               NIGERIA   • Mauritius
Ascension I.•

          SOUTH   NYASALAND
          WEST   RHODESIA
          AFRICA   SWAZILAND
St Helena• South African   BECHUANALAND
          mandate   BASUTOLAND
Tristan da Cunha•   SOUTH AFRICA

•• Falkland Is

● British Commonwealth
● British colonies and protectorates
○ British mandates
● Administered by the India Office

Total population of the British Empire 481,169,000

Africa 45,331,000
Europe 49,351,000   Asia 364,605,000
America 13,074,000   Oceania 8,808,000

37,000

Africa 2,093,000   Asia 1,971,000   Oceania 3,188,000
Europe 121,000

ures in square miles

Total land area of the British Empire 11,460,000 sq. miles

World War Two:
blitzkrieg

From the moment he came to power, Hitler concentrated on building up Germany's military strength. He aimed to recover all, and more than all, of the 1918 losses (see page 9). The Rhineland was re-occupied, union achieved with Austria, Czechoslovakia was crippled at Munich in 1938 and taken over in 1939. Poland was then ordered to hand over Danzig. These demands caused Britain to give Poland a guarantee against aggression. Hitler's reply was to announce a pact with Soviet Russia and to invade Poland on 1 September 1939. Two days later, Britain and France declared war on Germany. But they could do nothing to save Poland from being overwhelmed by the German *blitzkrieg* (lightning war).

It could be argued that the war would have occurred even if Hitler had never existed. Germany was still a young nation. Through her size and industrial skill, she was likely to become the strongest power on the European continent. If other nations denied her expansion, war was perhaps inevitable. Nazism, with its vicious racialism and extreme nationalism, added a new and terrible dimension to the German problem.

Adolf Hitler, the *Führer* (leader) of the German people. He gave them jobs, pride, discipline and success.
At the Munich Conference, his threats to Czechoslovakia paid off; Chamberlain, the British Prime Minister, gave in to his demands.

German Stuka, the *blitzkrieg* dive-bomber. It could dive down on a target and pull out almost at ground level.

Blitzkrieg

The Polish campaign was followed by the "phoney war", a lull, during which little happened until April 1940. Then, with dramatic suddenness, the Germans over-ran Norway and Denmark, took Holland and invaded Belgium.

With decisive aircraft support, their armoured columns swept across country at a speed which astonished the Allied generals. The Belgian Army surrendered, the French fell back in disarray and General Gort moved the British Army to the Channel coast.

From Dunkirk in northern France, more than 300,000 troops were brought home by the Royal Navy and a fleet of "little ships" that put out from England. All the army equipment was lost and France was left to her fate. Within ten days, Paris fell without resis-tance. On 22 June 1940, France surrendered.

Hitler had triumphed. In a matter of weeks, his invincible armies had over-run western Europe. Britain stood firm, but her army now had nothing to fight with. It only remained to destroy her air defences before launching an invasion.

On 8 August 1940, the Battle of Britain began. The Germans launched bomber attacks on shipping and fighter airfields. British fighters hit back, aided by the new radar stations. For the first time, the Germans had to face an efficient airforce.

The British Spitfires and Hurricanes inflicted such damage that, although the *Luftwaffe* (German airforce) continued its attacks into September, its losses were too heavy to be borne. By the end of the month, Hitler had called off the invasion.

German troops in Paris, 1940. They were to occupy northern France for the next four years.

Below: street battle in Russia. Hitler turned on Russia in 1941 and *blitzkrieg* tactics took the Germans to within 30 miles of Moscow.

1942 saw a drive to the south-east and a colossal struggle for Stalingrad. Here, in February 1943, the Germans were checked.

The Old Bailey law courts in ruins during the mass bombing of London. Known as the ''Blitz'', the bombing began as part of Hitler's invasion plans in 1940, but it continued long after the Battle of Britain. The attacks took place at night. People had to darken their windows and take refuge in shelters and Underground stations.

17

World War Two:
counterstrike

The United States entered the war after the Japanese attacked Pearl Harbour on 7 December 1941. Japan went on to win a series of striking victories throughout the Far East, but America, throwing all her vast resources into the struggle, set herself to recover the lost ground. Roosevelt decided that Germany was the main enemy and, after Montgomery had won the Battle of Alamein, American troops landed in North Africa. Together the Allies invaded Italy.

With the Russian victory at Stalingrad, the tide had turned. In June 1944, the Allies entered France. As the Russians drove westwards, a double advance pressed towards the heart of Germany. Rome, Paris, Kharkov, Brussels, Warsaw and Vienna fell. Though the Germans fought desperately, Berlin itself was captured. War in Europe ended in May 1945.

Meanwhile, the Americans had been recapturing island bases in the Pacific and had won major naval victories at Midway and Leyte Gulf. The scene was set for the invasion of Japan. It never occurred because, in August 1945, two atomic bombs brought about the Japanese surrender.

The surprise Japanese attack on the American naval base of Pearl Harbour, December 1941. Japan was friendly with Germany and entered the war unannounced.

British soldiers of the Eighth Army, the "Desert Rats", at the Battle of Alamein, October 1942. Montgomery's victory changed the course of the war.

War in the East

After Pearl Harbour, the Japanese over-ran the Pacific. They took Guam and Wake Island, Hong Kong, the Philippines, Singapore, the Dutch East Indies, Burma and most of New Guinea. India and Australia were now threatened by the enemy.

In June 1942, however, an American victory at Midway Island restored the naval balance. General MacArthur began "island hopping" towards Japan. After Admiral Halsey won the battle of Leyte Gulf in October 1944, MacArthur recaptured the Philippines and attacked Okinawa, close to Japan itself.

The Desert War

It was essential for Britain to maintain oil supplies, and so, vital that she held the Middle East. In 1940, General Wavell defeated Mussolini's army in North Africa. Hitler sent a brilliant general, Rommel, with a German army to help the Italians. By 1942, Rommel had advanced to the borders of Egypt.

The British situation was critical, but they took up a strong position at Alamein. Montgomery's victory was decisive. Rommel was driven back to Tunisia. By May 1943, the Allies' triumph was complete and they could concentrate their forces on Europe.

18

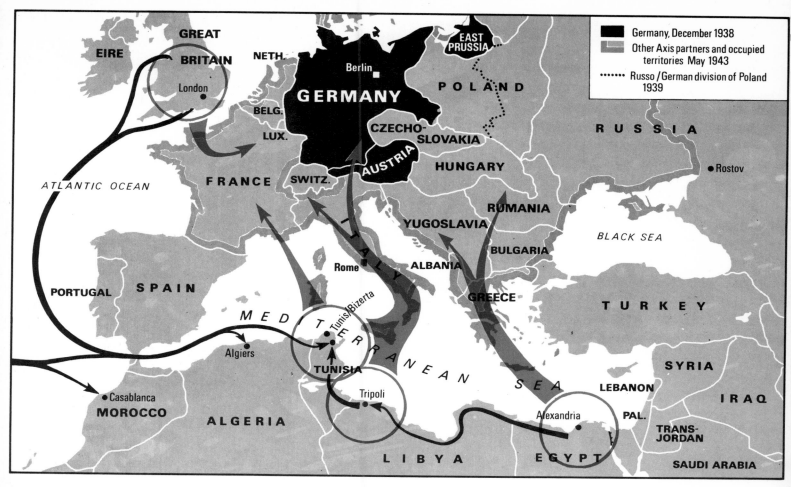

Counterstrike in Europe: the map shows how the Allies struck back at Germany from bases in North Africa and Britain. American and British troops landed at Casablanca and Algiers (November 1942) to join the victorious Eighth Army in Tunisia. Together, they invaded Sicily and Italy (September 1943).

From Britain, the Allies launched the Normandy invasion of June 1944. They entered southern France in August and Greece in October and drove up through the Balkans.

Notice the extent of the "Axis" (German-Italian) territories, stretching, at their height, from the Atlantic almost to Rostov.

The "Big Three" Allied leaders at Yalta in February 1945. Churchill (left) knew that Stalin (right) intended to take over Eastern Europe. Roosevelt (centre) was less suspicious of Russia. He felt that British imperialism would be a greater threat to peace once the war was over.

Surrender in Burma: a Japanese officer hands over his sword to the British.

On 6 August 1945, an American plane dropped one atomic bomb on Hiroshima, Japan's seventh largest city. Some 80,000 people were killed instantly. Three days later, a second bomb was dropped on Nagasaki.

So terrible was the destruction that the Japanese Emperor ordered his troops everywhere to lay down their arms.

How the Wars Compared

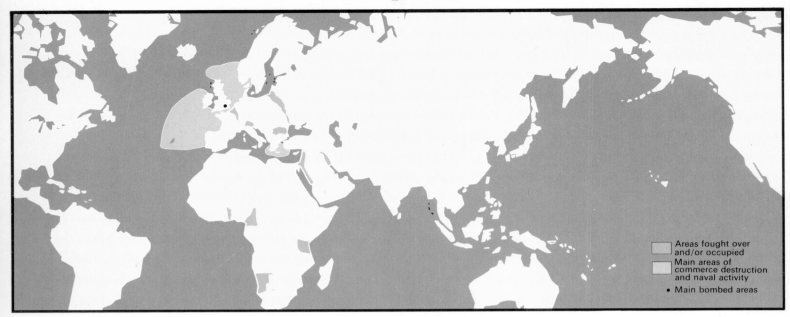

Map showing the extent of World War One. The main battle areas were northern France, South-East Europe, Russia and northern Italy. Minor campaigns took place in Africa and the Middle East.

Was World War Two merely a continuation of World War One? Certainly, the main contestants were the same—the British Commonwealth, France, Russia and America against Germany and Austria, joined, however, this time by Italy and Japan. Germany's desire for expansion was the same and her troops aimed to wipe out the defeat of 1918. As in the first war, victory went to the side that was able to turn out the most weapons and supplies.

But there were differences. In World War Two, Britain and France began reluctantly, not in the 1914 spirit of joyous heroism. Aircraft played a far bigger role, though bombing itself was not decisive until Hiroshima. It was a much more mobile war, with tanks and aircraft the key to success; much more a total war in which civilians often suffered worse than the soldiers; much more a world war in extent, in total cost and casualties.

Diagram showing casualties in World War One. The Commonwealth suffered more deaths in World War One because of the prolonged trench warfare. The economic cost was greater in World War Two, but sacrifices were more equally shared.

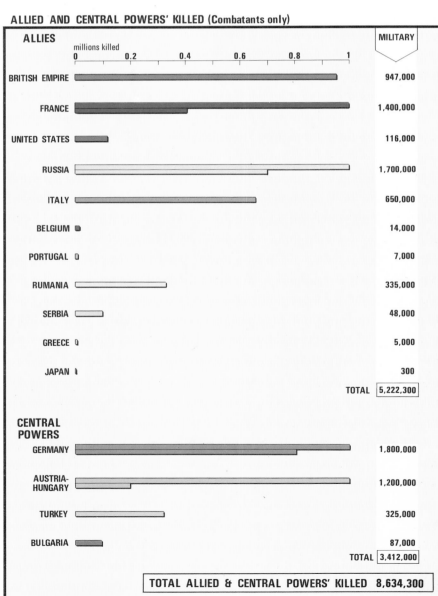

ALLIED AND CENTRAL POWERS' KILLED (Combatants only)

ALLIES	millions killed	MILITARY
BRITISH EMPIRE		947,000
FRANCE		1,400,000
UNITED STATES		116,000
RUSSIA		1,700,000
ITALY		650,000
BELGIUM		14,000
PORTUGAL		7,000
RUMANIA		335,000
SERBIA		48,000
GREECE		5,000
JAPAN		300
	TOTAL	5,222,300

CENTRAL POWERS		MILITARY
GERMANY		1,800,000
AUSTRIA-HUNGARY		1,200,000
TURKEY		325,000
BULGARIA		87,000
	TOTAL	3,412,000

TOTAL ALLIED & CENTRAL POWERS' KILLED 8,634,300

Legend (map):
- Areas fought over and/or occupied
- Main areas of commerce destruction and naval activity
- • Main bombed areas

World War Two extended across almost the whole of Europe, North Africa and South-East Asia. Britain, Germany and Japan were heavily bombed. The war at sea was fought mainly in the Atlantic and Pacific.

ALLIED AND AXIS KILLED (Combatants and civilians)

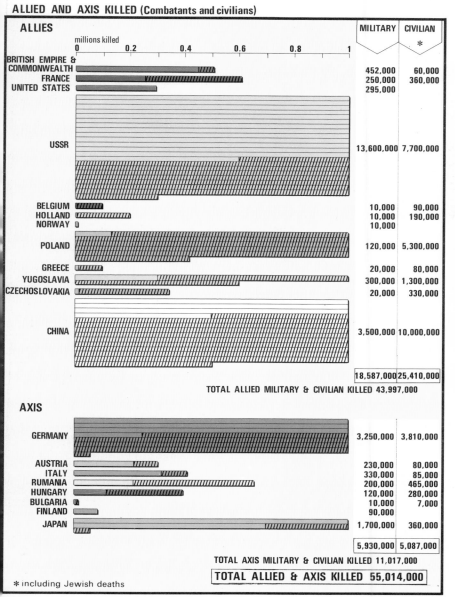

ALLIES	MILITARY	CIVILIAN *
BRITISH EMPIRE & COMMONWEALTH	452,000	60,000
FRANCE	250,000	360,000
UNITED STATES	295,000	
USSR	13,600,000	7,700,000
BELGIUM	10,000	90,000
HOLLAND	10,000	190,000
NORWAY	10,000	
POLAND	120,000	5,300,000
GREECE	20,000	80,000
YUGOSLAVIA	300,000	1,300,000
CZECHOSLOVAKIA	20,000	330,000
CHINA	3,500,000	10,000,000
	18,587,000	25,410,000

TOTAL ALLIED MILITARY & CIVILIAN KILLED 43,997,000

AXIS	MILITARY	CIVILIAN
GERMANY	3,250,000	3,810,000
AUSTRIA	230,000	80,000
ITALY	330,000	85,000
RUMANIA	200,000	465,000
HUNGARY	120,000	280,000
BULGARIA	10,000	7,000
FINLAND	90,000	
JAPAN	1,700,000	360,000
	5,930,000	5,087,000

TOTAL AXIS MILITARY & CIVILIAN KILLED 11,017,000

TOTAL ALLIED & AXIS KILLED 55,014,000

*including Jewish deaths

An American fighter-pilot in the Far East. Allied air superiority became a major factor in their victory.

Left: casualties in World War Two. They were far heavier overall than in the first war.

The scale and fury of the fighting on the Russian front was tremendous. There was mass extermination of civilians in occupied countries, including millions of Jews. Chinese civilian casualties were caused by Japanese barbarity, civil war and famine.

21

Civilians at War

The British public did not welcome war in 1939 with the flag-waving patriotism of 1914. Their mood was much more grim and realistic. They knew that this would be a people's war in which civilians would have to suffer and serve like the fighting men. From the outset, the government managed things far more efficiently; men and women were called up to serve in the forces and in industry in an orderly fashion. When peace came, there was no near-mutiny over demobilization as there had been after World War One. Food, clothing, furniture and fuel were rationed with remarkable fairness and special provision was made to keep expectant mothers and children healthy. The Blitz made people feel that they were all engaged in the struggle, all in the same boat. The nation was united as never before or since.

It was total war, yet at home, people were more civilized than in 1914–18. There was little victimization of conscientious objectors, no handing out of white feathers, the mark of disgrace, or banning of German composers.

Britons queueing for a "No Conscription" meeting during World War One. Until 1916, all servicemen volunteered.

Below: Boy Scouts helping out with the harvest, World War One. Young people helped the national effort.

SOUTH AUSTRALIANS

COO-EE!

FALL IN!

WE WANT YOU AT THE FRONT

COME AND HELP ENLIST AT ONCE

Australian recruiting poster of World War One. To the surprise of the Germans and Americans, the Empire came readily to Britain's aid. Canada, Australia and New Zealand raised armies; even Boers in South Africa put aside old quarrels. Supposedly oppressed peoples like the Indians and Irish volunteered to fight.

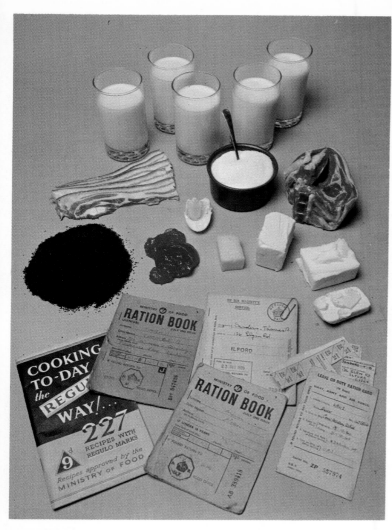

World War Two: some of the thousands of children who were evacuated from big cities to "safe areas". Most soon returned home.

Left: a week's rations for one person during World War Two. Food was fairly shared. Notice the half-egg and tiny piece of cheese.

Below: gas-mask drill. Expecting gas attacks, the government issued gas-masks to everyone in Britain.

Women Fight for Freedom

One of the most striking features of the 20th century has been the increased part that women play in society. In Britain, until the middle of the last century, they had no right to vote, to enter universities or the professions, or to own property. They could not keep their earnings, or even their children if their husband chose to leave or divorce them. By 1914, some of these wrongs had been corrected but people's attitudes were hard to change. Women were looked on as either refined helpless creatures or as household drudges whose job was to bear children and mind the home. The idea of a woman competing with men on equal terms was regarded as ludicrous, a point of view which most women accepted.

Women were given the vote in 1918 in Britain, and 1920 in America. Two world wars, education and full employment have brought enormous changes in attitudes towards women's rights and such questions as divorce, equal pay and careers for married women. Even so, some people feel that women are still badly off, and that much remains to be done before people recognize that men and women are truly equal.

British suffragette is removed from a political meeting.

Suffragettes

The Suffragette movement was founded in 1903 by Christabel Pankhurst and her mother, Emmeline, to give women the vote. Their supporters were mostly upper-class ladies and, from heckling politicians and chaining themselves to railings, they adopted more militant protests.

They broke windows, set fire to houses and slashed valuable pictures. Some went to prison and those who went on hunger-strike were forcibly fed. On the outbreak of World War One, Mrs Pankhurst called off the campaign.

Left: an Edwardian "New Woman".

Women keyboard operators in a printing works, 1911. Women could now get jobs that were better paid and less tyrannical than domestic service. Women could also be trained as teachers and nurses.

The "New Woman" had appeared before women were given the vote.

British girls humping coal during World War One. "Let us prove ourselves worthy of citizenship whether our claim is recognized or not," said one leading suffragette.

Women's contribution to the war effort led directly to their emancipation in 1918.

American "flappers" in the 1920's. Emancipated women rejoiced in their new freedom.

They cut their hair short, smoked, wore lipstick and "daring" clothes. More important was the general acceptance of women having careers and independence.

Mrs Indira Gandhi became Prime Minister of India in 1966. She is the leader of over 500 million people.

Left: a mother with her hungry children during the Depression in America. Although a woman now has virtually the same rights as a man, she is still wife and mother, usually bearing the brunt of family duties and anxieties.

Often she is dependent upon her husband for money. Some Women's Liberation supporters want to see housewives paid a proper wage for the jobs they do.

25

Road Transport

When the 20th century opened, the roads were used almos entirely by horse-drawn traffic. There were motorists, but the were a small class of wealthy enthusiasts. The rest of the popu lation went about in carriages, pony-traps, horse-drawn buses on bicycles or on foot.

Thanks to Henry Ford's mass production techniques, Amer ica was the first country to produce cars which the ordinar man could afford (see page 74). Between the wars, Willian Morris and Herbert Austin brought motoring within the reacl of the British middle classes. Public transport in the form c buses, trams, trolley-buses and underground trains provided an efficient service for most people. Since World War Two, al industrialized countries have seen a tremendous increase in th number of car owners. This has produced employment pleasure and convenience for millions of people but it has als brought about a marked decline in public transport. Cars hav brought a new pollution problem, and made the old problen of over-crowding in cities worse. As the world's oil supplie diminish, the motor car's hey-day may already be over.

Public transport
The picture shows a pre-1914 motor bus of the General Omni-bus Company; note the solid tyres and open top deck. There is no windscreen (in wet weather, the driver and passengers on top were given waterproof aprons).

From 1905, London's horse-drawn buses were converted by having petrol engines fitted to them. The last horse-bus vanished from the streets in 1911. Electric trains carried more passengers than the buses and tramway mile-age in Britain doubled between 1900 and 1907.

These forms of public trans-

Bus, and early bus-ticket with an advertisement on the back.

port, with the newly opened tube trains, led to a great expansion of suburban areas. People could now live further from their work, travelling in and out of cities every day.

The Family Car

Since the car's invention in the 19th century, manufacturers vied with each other in producing luxurious models for the wealthy.

Then, men like Ford, Morris and Austin realized that vast profits could be made from producing family cars on a large scale.

The ordinary man wanted a car that was cheap and reliable. The Model "T" Ford and Austin 7 fitted the bill. These and later family cars had bodies as roomy as possible to take passengers and luggage, with engines giving a moderate performance and consuming little petrol.

British Austin 7 saloon, 1929. It cost about £160, with a running cost of ½p per mile.

The "Baby Austin" was first produced as an open model in 1922 and it brought motoring within reach of people with modest incomes.

William Morris countered with the Morris Minor, said to do 100 miles to the gallon!

KEEP DEATH OFF THE ROAD
CARELESSNESS KILLS

British Road Safety Poster of 1948. It was withdrawn because people found it too depressing. Yet it was meant to shock motorists, for thousands are killed on the roads every year.

A "spaghetti junction": a network of freeways in Los Angeles. Road-building seldom keeps pace with the increase in traffic.

The B.M.C. Mini, the brilliant creation of designer Alec Issigonis.

Reliable, nippy, easy to park and cheap to run, it seats four persons and appeals to almost every class of motorist; it is specially useful in towns and for people who do comparatively short journeys.

American Motors Javelin S.S.T., 1971. American cars have generally been bigger than British cars, chiefly because petrol has been cheaper. Parking problems and the oil shortage may reverse this trend.

Cinema

The great era of silent films lasted for barely two decades. Only two of its stars, Garbo and Chaplin, survived the arrival of the "talkies" with *The Jazz Singer* in 1927. Yet the silent screen set the style of the film industry and established Hollywood as the centre for film-making. There followed a golden age in the 1930's, when cinema drew almost everyone like a magnet. Hollywood turned out a stream of dazzling productions—westerns and gangster films, musicals and cartoons, romance, comedy, and, occasionally, social comment (*The Grapes of Wrath* and *Citizen Kane*, for example).

Casablanca and *Brief Encounter* were two fine films which appeared during World War Two, and Hollywood brought out big musicals and spectaculars in the 1950's to compete with television. Yet, despite advances like cinerama, and gimmicks like 3-D films, audiences declined. Gifted European directors, using new styles and techniques, challenged the American industry. Television has now replaced cinema as the main form of popular entertainment, yet films still attract a devoted following, particularly among young people.

Above: silent film slide warns of peril in the dark! Right: Chaplin in *Work* (1915) with Edna Purviance.

The Silent Screen

Film-making began at the turn of the century with short comic tales and vaudeville acts. Then came the first full-length "story", *The Great Train Robbery*, in 1903. California's sunny climate was perfect for filming, and, when war broke out in Europe, American know-how made Hollywood supreme.

From 1914, Hollywood produced hundreds of films—slap-stick with Chaplin and Keaton, epics like *Intolerance* and romantic adventures with Douglas Fairbanks, Mary Pickford and Rudolph Valentino. The only sounds were provided by pianists in the cinema itself. The story was conveyed in short captions flashed onto the screen.

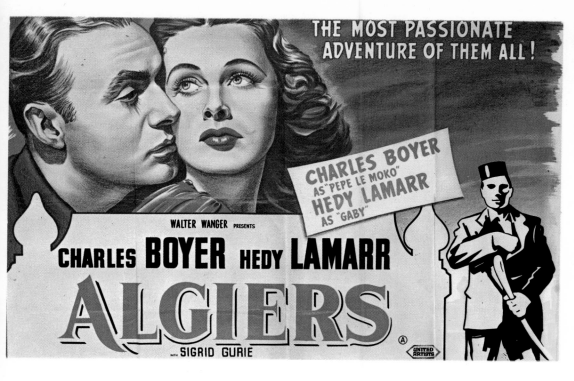

THE MOST PASSIONATE ADVENTURE OF THEM ALL!

CHARLES BOYER AS "PEPE LE MOKO"
HEDY LAMARR AS "GABY"

WALTER WANGER PRESENTS

CHARLES **BOYER** HEDY **LAMARR**

ALGIERS

WITH SIGRID GURIE

UNITED ARTISTS

Film poster of the 1930's shows Charles Boyer and Hedy Lamarr in *Algiers*. Other foreign stars included Greta Garbo, Ingmar Bergman and Marlene Dietrich. Although Hollywood was the centre for making films, many of the stars, particularly those who played exotic and romantic roles, came from abroad.

The leading American stars were Clark Gable, Spencer Tracy, James Cagney, Gary Cooper, Katharine Hepburn, Ginger Rogers and Joan Crawford British stars included Fred Astaire, Ronald Colman and Charles Laughton.

Among the outstanding films of the 1930's were *Grand Hotel*, *Gone with the Wind* and *A Night at the Opera*.

Mickey Mouse and Donald Duck on a magazine cover, 1937. Animated films began with simple outline figures like Felix the Cat. Between the wars, Walt Disney's cartoons sparkled with charm and originality. In 1938, he made his first full-length cartoon in colour, *Snow White and the Seven Dwarfs*. Other cartoon extravaganzas followed, but some feel that these later films were marred by sentimentality.

Modern cartoons like *Yellow Submarine* (1968) employ a fresher approach, sometimes using photographs as well as hand-drawn figures.

Marlon Brando in *A Streetcar Named Desire* (1951). He was one of the new ''method'' actors (Paul Newman and Rod Steiger were two others). They involved themselves completely in their roles for the sake of realism.

Scene from *The Andromeda Strain*, a modern science fiction film. Since the early days of the cinema, with *The Cabinet of Doctor Caligari* (1919), fantasy and horror films have been great favourites.

The Shrinking World

Telegraph systems had been set up in America and Britain by the 1850's and the first Transatlantic cable was laid in 1858. The telephone made its appearance in 1876, but long distance services were not efficient until the turn of the century. Since that time, telephones have become an indispensable method of communication. Through automatic exchanges, electronic computers, radio links and telex systems, messages can now be relayed across the world.

Two other forms of communication which affect all our lives, radio and television, also had their beginnings in the last century. Yet radio broadcasts did not begin until 1920, and although Baird had demonstrated television by this time, the first television service did not begin until 1936. For entertainment and information, radio (or "wireless" as it was then called) reigned supreme between the wars and on until the early 1950's. Since then, television has taken over. Both have helped to create a "mass culture"—a world in which millions may hear or see the same programmes, pick up the same fashions, even think the same thoughts.

General Post Office telephone, 1902. London's first telephone exchange opened in 1879; the Post Office took over the National Telephone Company in 1912 and was operating a million telephones by 1920. In America, the systems have always been privately owned.

Harry Tate, the famous music-hall comedian, broadcasts in 1923.

Radio

Broadcasting began in America in 1920 and the British Broadcasting Company was formed two years later. Britain, unlike America, had no commercial radio for 50 years.

By the 1930's, the golden age of sound broadcasting, almost everyone listened nightly to the "wireless". During the war, radio united and heartened Britain through music, news, Churchill's speeches and comedy programmes like *ITMA* (*It's That Man Again*). Transistors were invented in 1948; radios could now be carried anywhere.

Diagram showing the effect of television on cinema-going in Britain.

At the top, television licences can be seen to rise from virtually none in 1950 to 15 million in 1968. At the same time, cinema-goers have shrunk from 28·6 million to 4·4 million.

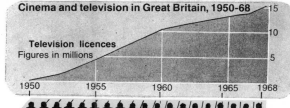

Cinema and television in Great Britain, 1950-68

Television licences
Figures in millions

1950 1955 1960 1965 1968

6.1 5.4 5.0 4.4
7.6 6.8 6.5
10.0 8.7
11.5
15.0
18.3
23.9 22.2
25.8
28.0 26.8 26.2
28.6

Right: Julie Andrews on American colour television, 1959.

J. L. Baird, who pioneered television in the 1920's, showed that colour was a possibility but it only became common in America in the 1950's, and in Britain from 1967.

Below: apparatus for communicating with Telstar, Seattle, 1963.

Radio waves are restricted by the curvature of the earth. However, if a relay station is placed high above the earth, signals can be bounced off it to cover a wide area.

This was done in 1962 when television transmissions were made via the American satellite, Telstar.

Music for All

Until this century, most people had to make their own music or hire musicians to play for them. Radios, gramophones and tape-recorders have now made it possible for ordinary people to hear huge orchestras in the comfort of their own homes.

Thomas Edison invented the gramophone in 1877, and commercial recording was established in 1890. By 1925, when electrical recording was introduced, most popular singers and much orchestral music were available on record. Tape-recorders and long-playing records appeared after World War Two. People could now hear long passages of music without the nuisance of having to turn records over.

Millions now enjoy Mozart and Beethoven. Yet today's composers have become "difficult" to most people. "Concrete" musicians question what "music" really means. If the sound of a violin string vibrating is musical, why not the squeak of a tape played backwards, or the sound of traffic? Music-lovers of the future may accept their experiments, but, for the moment, record-buyers have preferred classical music, ballads, the swing of jazz or the pounding rhythms of rock and roll.

Marie Lloyd, a great star of the music-halls.
 Music-halls were the centres for popular music in the Edwardian Age. They offered a cheap evening's entertainment of bawdy and sentimental songs. With the growth of the cinema, many music-hall stars left the stage for the screen.

Right: a "flapper" of the 1920's does the Charleston. With new methods of mass communications, dance-fads like the Charleston, Jive and Twist have swept the world with incredible speed throughout the century.

32

New Music

In 1913, Stravinsky's *Rite of Spring* opened in Paris to a stormy reception. It seemed to have no tune or harmony, and the bewildered audience reacted with boos and catcalls. The music is now a popular concert piece.

Composers have experimented with new forms throughout the 20th century, and it often takes a long time before the public comes to appreciate them.

Dancers in the ballet *Rite of Spring*. The choreography was by Diaghilev.

The Beatles, from left to right, Paul, George, Ringo and John. They shot to fame in 1963.

Bob Dylan at the Isle of Wight Pop Festival, 1969. He brought poetry and social issues to pop music.

Pop Music

During the first quarter of the century, people began to hear a new kind of music—jazz. It was based on the spirituals sung by American Negroes, but given a hectic rhythm that echoed the pace of city life. Jazz is the root of modern pop music.

In the 1950's, singers like Elvis Presley and Chuck Berry adapted jazz with twanging electric guitars and a thumping drum-beat. They reached a vast, international "teenage" audience that now had more money to spend on clothes, records and transistor radios.

In the 1960's, the Beatles and the Rolling Stones astonished the adult world with their long hair and rebellious attitudes. Pop stars came to influence young people's opinions. Bob Dylan, for example, wrote songs of protest against racial injustice and nuclear warfare.

33

Science and Technology

It has been said that out of all the scientists that have ever lived, nine out of ten are alive today. The 20th century has brought a massive increase in the amounts of money that governments spend on scientific research. "Technology" is the practical application of scientific principles. It has revolutionized society. Machines increasingly take over the work of men. New materials such as nylons and other plastics have transformed clothes and household goods. Fantastically shaped buildings can be made with "pre-stressed" concrete. Cars become faster, weapons become deadlier.

Science itself has changed our view of the world. Men like Einstein and Rutherford gave us the new science of nuclear physics in the first half of the century. In the 1950's, Watson and Crick discovered D.N.A.; we now have a better understanding of how our bodies grow, and how characteristics are passed on from one generation to another. Today, radio telescopes can locate worlds that are millions of miles away. Field-ion microscopes can show the positions of atoms, which are millions of times smaller than a pin-head.

Albert Einstein (1879–1955).

Nuclear Physics

Newton, in the 17th century, believed that the world was made up of "atoms", which he described as tiny, hard balls. His view was widely held until this century, when scientists have shown that atoms consist mostly of empty space with a "nucleus" of "protons" and "neutrons" in the centre. The protons in the nucleus have a positive electrical charge. Much smaller "electrons", with a negative electrical charge, can be found in an area around the nucleus.

The nucleus can be split in a process called nuclear fission. When a nucleus is split, a certain amount of it simply disappears and becomes energy. Splitting the atom has lead to peaceful uses of "nuclear" energy, but also to the horror of the "atomic" bomb.

Below: original chamber with which Chadwick discovered the neutron in 1932. Scientists discovered that atoms could be split if they were bombarded with neutrons.

Computers

Above: an IBM 360/75 computer. Computers are machines that can handle symbols—letters or numbers, for example. They can calculate at superhuman speeds, or store vast amounts of information in tiny "memory cells".

Since the 1950's, they have become indispensable in business and communications. Yet scientists disagree about the future. Will computers ever be able to "think" like human beings?

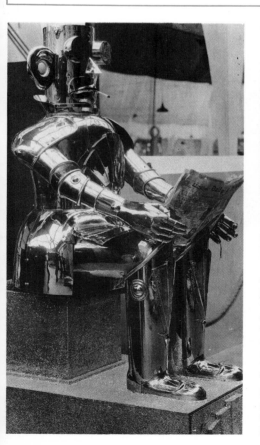

Above: cartoon of "automation" — man seems to have become a mechanical slave to his creations. Automation means making machines or processes automatic, so that they need little or no human supervision. Left: a "friendly robot" at the 1932 Radio Show, Earls Court, London. This is a simple view of automation. In fact, the "automatic pilot" of a modern aircraft, or an "automatic" washing machine, need not look human to do a human's work.

A new wonder of modern science; the laser-beam. The laser was developed by Charles Townes and Arthur Schwalow in the 1950's. The American scientist Theodore Maiman produced the first working model in California in 1960.

Laser-beams are intense beams of light. They can pierce holes in metal and even jewels. They are so precise that they can be used for delicate surgical operations. They are also used for communications.

Weapons Grow Deadlier

Since the beginning of history, victory in war has always gone to the side with the more effective weapons. Iron was better than bronze; cannons replaced longbows; rifles replaced muskets. The pace of advance quickened in the 19th century, when machine guns, high explosives and long-range artillery arrived. Inventors devised torpedoes, mines and submarines that were to change the pattern of naval war.

In two world wars and in later wars like Vietnam, weapons became infinitely more deadly through the close association of scientists with the military leaders. In World War One, co-operation was often lacking. New weapons like poison gas and tanks failed to make a decisive impact, at least at first. Both sides learnt the lesson. In World War Two, scientific research produced radar, explosives of unparalleled power, pilotless aircraft, the V2 rocket and the ultimate horror of the atomic bomb. Modern war can be waged with such ghastly weapons as chemicals that destroy vegetation, bacteria that spread disease, and napalm, a jelly fuel that is used in incendiary bombs and flame-throwers.

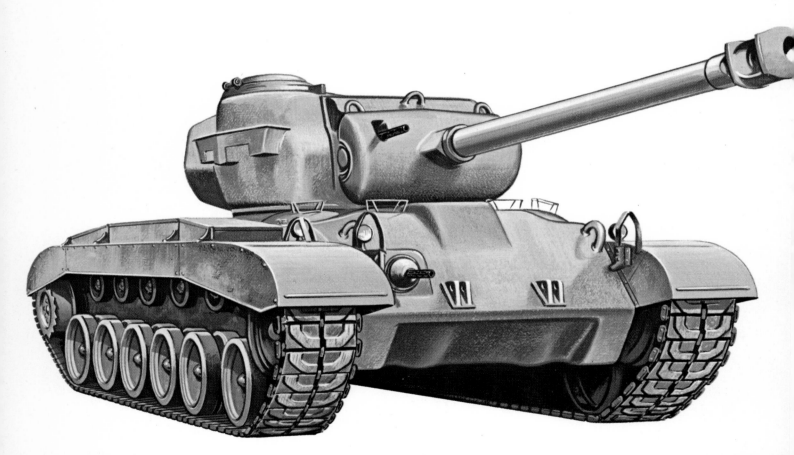

The Story of the Tank

Tanks developed from the idea of a British officer, Colonel Swinton, to build a tracked vehicle that would break the stalemate of trench warfare. The name "tank" was a codeword to deceive the enemy.

Despite the scepticism of most generals, the new tanks made a dramatic advance at Cambrai in 1917, though lack of reserves prevented a breakthrough. In 1918, however, tanks became a decisive factor in the Allied victory.

Between the wars, German experts gave much thought to tank warfare. The outcome of their theories was seen in the *blitzkrieg*, when massed tank columns, closely supported by aircraft, swept across Poland and France.

Like aircraft, tanks became abso-

Pershing T-25 E1, considered the best and most modern American tank of World War Two.

lutely essential for defence and attack. In North Africa, Russia and across Europe, victory came to depend upon "armour" and its tactical use. It became vital to maintain good fuel supplies.

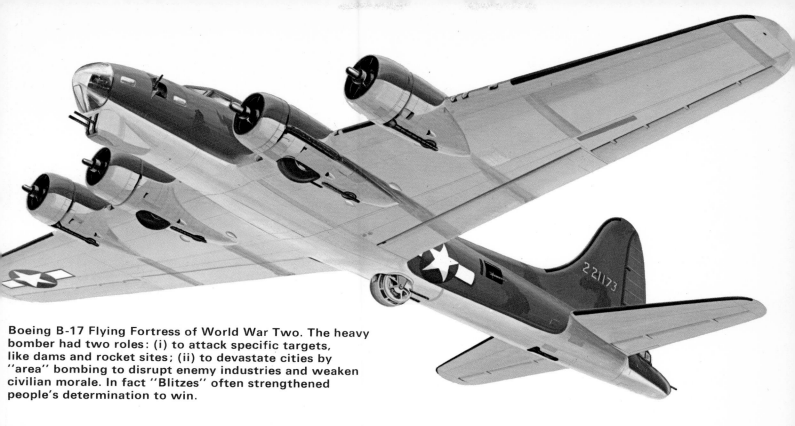

Boeing B-17 Flying Fortress of World War Two. The heavy bomber had two roles: (i) to attack specific targets, like dams and rocket sites; (ii) to devastate cities by "area" bombing to disrupt enemy industries and weaken civilian morale. In fact "Blitzes" often strengthened people's determination to win.

Panel of A.S.V. (Air to Surface Vessel) radar. It allowed bombers to detect surfaced U-boats.

Radar

Radar was developed in Britain before World War Two. It was first used to detect the approach of enemy aircraft.

A powerful transmitter on the ground sent out radio waves which, on striking an aircraft, sent back an echo to a receiver. It became possible to calculate the aircraft's position and speed.

Later, it became possible to install radar sets in aircraft for interception, navigation, and target identification (radar could "see" the ground below). Radar was used in ships to detect other vessels, in tanks and for artillery.

A modern Titan II rocket, a powerful American inter-continental missile, bursts from its underground silo.

The forerunner of ballistic missiles was the German V2 rocket, used against England in 1944. 50 ft (15·2 m) long, with a one-ton warhead, it flew at three times the speed of sound and had a 200-mile range.

There was no answer to it but to capture the launching sites. If German scientists had produced it earlier, it could have changed the outcome of the war.

The Shadow of the Bomb

In 1945, the United States alone possessed the atomic bomb, and with it, the power to defeat any country in the world. Stalin was concerned to protect Russia from attack by the West. He speedily saw to it that practically every state in Eastern Europe had a Communist government. By 1949, Russia had also produced her own nuclear weapon. America was alarmed by the spread of Communism, and had announced, in the "Truman Doctrine" of 1947, that she would aid free peoples if they were threatened by armed minorities.

This was the beginning of the "Cold War", a state of hostility between East and West just short of actual fighting. Wars in Korea and Vietnam have nearly brought the armies of the major powers to direct clashes, a crisis over Cuba almost brought about a nuclear war. In the city of Berlin, divided after World War Two, a single wall separates the two camps.

East and West keep perpetual watch on each other through spies, aerial and submarine reconnaissance. Both keep their deadly weapons poised to strike. Both compete relentlessly for the friendship of the smaller nations.

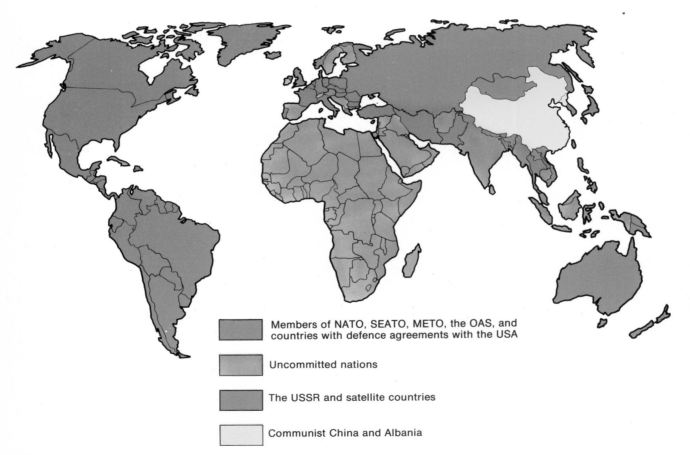

Members of NATO, SEATO, METO, the OAS, and countries with defence agreements with the USA

Uncommitted nations

The USSR and satellite countries

Communist China and Albania

The Balance of Power
By 1948, Russia, Poland, East Germany, Bulgaria, Czechoslovakia, Yugoslavia, Hungary, Rumania and Albania were Communist.

The United States, Britain and France formed N.A.T.O. (North Atlantic Treaty Organization) for defence against aggression. N.A.T.O. came to include Canada and most of Western Europe.

O.A.S. (Organization of American States) brought Latin America into the camp and S.E.A.T.O. (South-East Asia Treaty Organization) included Australasia, Pakistan and the Philippines. M.E.T.O. (Middle East Treaty Organization) linked N.A.T.O. and S.E.A.T.O.

Russia countered these alliances with the Warsaw Pact for defence of the Communist states.

Above: defensive alliances after World War Two.

Right: British nuclear explosion at Maralinga, Australia, 1956 (Britain had joined the U.S. and Russia in producing atomic bombs).
This blast, equivalent to perhaps 20,000 tons of T.N.T., was a small one; explosions thousands of times stronger were made later. The atomic bomb could probably destroy all life on this planet.

The American Dream

Vast natural resources, energy, get-ahead business methods and a generally willing labour force have made America the richest country on earth. Her wealth has become a by-word. Her way of life is copied throughout the English-speaking world and beyond. American power decided two world wars; American aid twice enabled Europe to recover from its folly. The "Marshall Plan" (1948–52) pumped $13,150 million into Europe to help recovery. No country in history has been as generous as America to its friends and former enemies.

For more than three centuries, America was the land of opportunity. To millions who were poor and oppressed, it stood for freedom and equality. Roosevelt expressed the American ideal in his declaration of the four freedoms—freedom of speech, freedom of worship, freedom from want and freedom from fear. Yet these were an ideal to be aimed for, not a reality. While Americans strode confidently into the second half of the century, doubts began to arise. People became more aware of the poverty, slums, violence and pollution that exist in this land of plenty.

Douglas Fairbanks and Mary Pickford ("the World's Sweetheart"), stars of the silent screen in the 1920's.

From the start, Hollywood films showed America as glamorous and exciting. American films influenced fashion and, with the coming of the "talkies", speech.

Joseph Kennedy, ambassador to Britain 1938–40, with his sons, Edward, John, Joseph and Robert.

Descendants of poor immigrants, the Kennedys became wealthy and powerful in a single generation. But they were tragically unlucky; Joseph was killed in the war; John, President of the U.S., and Robert, a senator, were assassinated.

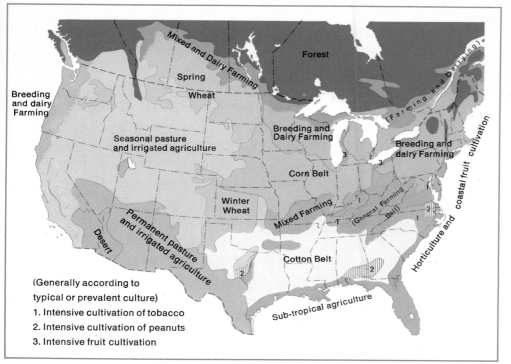

(Generally according to typical or prevalent culture)
1. Intensive cultivation of tobacco
2. Intensive cultivation of peanuts
3. Intensive fruit cultivation

Continent and Country

The sheer size of the United States makes it a continent; the state of California is bigger than Italy or Japan, Texas is larger than France. The Mid-West, the South, the industrial North-East, the Pacific states and the Rockies are regions as different from each other as, say, Norway is from Spain.

States vary in climate, occupations, racial origins and political leanings. Yet, out of these differences, a nation has been formed with a common way of life and a remarkable unity.

Left: agricultural regions of the United States.

Below: the big car, symbol of America's industrial prosperity (a Pontiac advertisement, 1956).

America in Search of a Role

At the end of World War Two, the instinct of President Truman and many Americans was to "bring the boys home" and have done with far-off problems. "Isolationism" had won the day after 1918 and it was still strong. But America was too powerful to opt out of world affairs. Roosevelt's good will towards Stalin gave way to a more realistic attitude, as Truman, Marshall and Dean Acheson came to see the Russian threat. When, in 1947, Britain announced that she could no longer aid Greece and Turkey to stem Communism, America stepped in. By the Truman Doctrine, she would help free countries to resist being taken over. The Marshall Programme was launched to give aid to war-damaged nations in the belief that Communism would not flourish in prosperous societies.

America's policy was not to win back countries which had succumbed, but to prevent Communism spreading further. Latin America and South-East Asia were key areas. When North Korean Communists invaded South Korea, United Nations forces, mostly American, were sent in. For similar reasons, America became tragically involved in Vietnam.

Above: early American General Motors car factory in Uruguay.

Below: hostile reception in Venezuela for Richard Nixon on a tour of Latin America. American influence has sometimes provoked dislike.

ARTZYBASHEFF

A satirical view of "Americanization". The thirsty world is being wooed with Coca-Cola.

The world received more than 40,000 million dollars-worth of non-military aid between 1945 and 1965. This generosity provides staggering proof that American governments really believe in rich nations helping the poorer ones.

Vietnam

By 1954, Vietnam had thrown off French rule. Liberation was won by North Vietnamese Communists, aided by China. The country was then divided into two hostile states, the Communist North and the Nationalist South. From 1959, northern and local Communists became active in the South.

When it seemed likely to collapse, President Johnson sent U.S. forces and ordered bombing attacks on the North. From 1964, America became embroiled in a savage jungle war. As hopes of a swift victory receded, public opinion became bitterly hostile. Peace was signed in 1973, but the situation remained chaotic.

War in Vietnam: wounded soldiers are taken out of the battle zone.

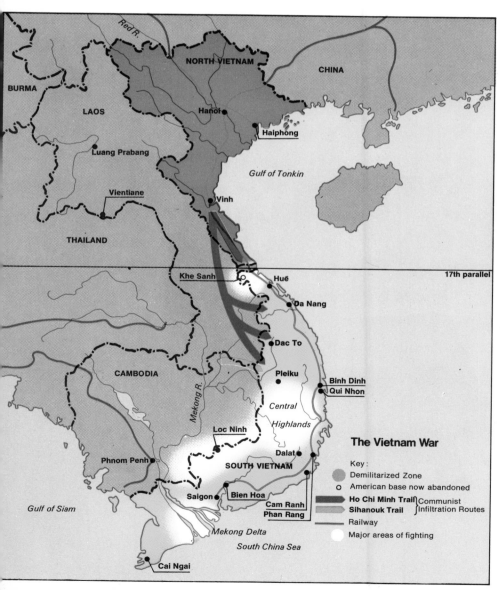

The Vietnam War

Key:
- Demilitarized Zone
- ○ American base now abandoned
- **Ho Chi Minh Trail** — Communist Infiltration Routes
- **Sihanouk Trail**
- Railway
- ○ Major areas of fighting

Vietnam, 1969: North and South are joined by a narrow coastal strip. Enmity existed centuries before the present conflict.

Cartoon pointing out the hazards of assistance to foreign peoples. The American way is not necessarily suitable elsewhere.

Americans have ruefully discovered that giving aid often earns resentment abroad and at home, especially when (as in Vietnam) it leads to disastrous involvement.

Crime and Violence

One of the more baffling features of our time is that, as people become better-off, crime and violence seem to increase rather than diminish. Statistics suggest that Britain was much more law-abiding in the days of mass poverty and unemployment. Even the shoot-ups in America's Wild West were tame compared with the violence that Prohibition bred, or the "muggings" that daily occur in America's big cities.

In rich societies, student and race riots, and violent picketing take place. Vandalism has become commonplace. New crimes, such as the hijacking of aircraft have occurred. Criminal groups such as the Mafia have organized their activities on a massive scale. The world has grown kinder towards the unfortunate, the handicapped and the offender. Yet, strangely, it has grown ever more violent.

Vandalism: children and broken windows on a housing estate. Parks, schools and railways are regular targets for attack. Some people believe that the pressures of modern city life cause vandalism.

Are children taking revenge on an adult world which both cossets and neglects them? Do they need more playgrounds, or more thrashing?

Right: a skit on the sensational "tabloid" newspapers which became popular in the 1920's.

Many people hold that constantly seeing violence in the press, in films and on television breeds a love of violence. Even westerns, and cartoons like "Tom and Jerry" have come under criticism.

Others say that violence must be shown realistically, since it is a part of our lives. Film and T.V. producers also say that they are giving the public what it likes; thrillers and "heroes" like James Bond.

Prohibition

Alcohol was illegal from 1920 to 1933 in the United States. This "prohibition" gave rise to gangsterism and to corruption of police, politicians and even judges.

Worse, it corrupted the public by inducing contempt for the law. Almost everyone broke the liquor

End of a gangster – the body of Frank Yale, Mafia chief and liquor boss, murdered by Al Capone's gang.

regulations and criminals like Al Capone went unmolested. By tradition, anyone can carry a gun in America and violence has always been a fact of life.

Preparing a marijuana cigarette. Drug-taking has become a problem all over the world.

Drugs are generally considered to be harmful, some disastrously so, and they cause large numbers of people to defy the law. Crime may be committed by persons affected by drugs or needing supplies.

John F. Kennedy in a small town during his victorious Presidential campaign in 1960.

His election brought to the White House a young man who radiated energy and charm. He promised America a "New Frontier", where concern for the quality of life would replace greed for material things.

He would tackle problems that had been neglected – health, welfare, education, racial discrimination – in the hope of creating a more just society.

It was a brilliant beginning but it came to a tragic end.

Death of a President

In 1963, President Kennedy was making a tour of Texas. On 22 November, accompanied by his wife and Governor Connally, he drove through Dallas in an open car. An unseen assassin fired two shots and the President died almost immediately.

An ex-Marine named Lee Harvey Oswald was arrested, only to be shot dead, whilst in police custody. Oswald's murderer was an odd character, Jack Ruby, who declared that he killed Oswald because he was enraged by the assassination.

It was widely rumoured, however, that there had been a plot to kill Kennedy. Perhaps the shooting was the work of more than one man, and Ruby had shot Oswald to silence him? The Warren Commission, set up to discover the truth, reported that Oswald was the sole assassin and that there was no conspiracy. Although most people accepted these findings, the whole episode remains mysterious.

Assassination was not new in America; Kennedy was the fourth President to die in this manner. His brother Robert was shot dead in 1968, and Martin Luther King, the Negro leader, was killed in the same year.

Prison: haircutting day at Wormwood Scrubs. Prison reform continues to aim at "rehabilitating" the offender (fitting him into society) through training and parole. The work is hampered by overcrowding and out-of-date buildings.

Race in America

Slavery was prohibited in 1863 and, for a time after the Civil War, Negroes were able to vote and stand for representative office. But the southern whites soon recovered their position. By the early 1900's, Negroes had been effectively excluded from public life. Segregation laws and the Ku Klux Klan kept them in a lowly position.

As the map on the right shows, Negroes began to move from the South to the industrial North. There they found work, usually unskilled, and made their homes in run-down city centres. Conditions were often appalling. Nevertheless, they continued to come and, by the 1960's, nearly half of the Negro population was living in the North.

Protests for equal civil rights began in the South and the Negroes found a national leader in Martin Luther King. Meanwhile, in the North, protest took a more extreme form as the Black Power movement made itself felt. America is a nation of many peoples. Since the 1960's, other racial groups—Indians, Puerto Ricans, Mexican and Spanish Americans, are also becoming vocal in their demands for equality.

**Above: a Mohawk Indian construction worker today.
Right: an Indian tepee sited in Washington in 1968 as a protest against the loss of Indian lands.**

By 1900, barely a quarter of a million Indians were left. Most of them lived in reservations as poor "second-class citizens".

However, by 1970, their numbers had trebled and they were drawing attention to their grievances.

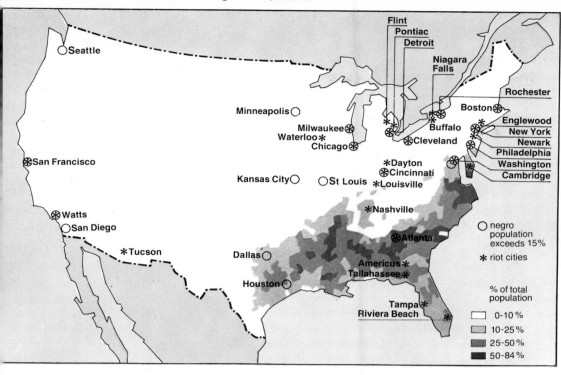

Seattle
Flint
Pontiac
Detroit
Niagara Falls
Rochester
Minneapolis
Boston
Milwaukee
Waterloo
Chicago
Buffalo
Cleveland
Englewood
New York
Newark
Philadelphia
Washington
Cambridge
San Francisco
Kansas City
St Louis
Dayton
Cincinnati
Louisville
Watts
Nashville
San Diego
Tucson
Atlanta
Dallas
Americus
Tallahassee
Houston
Tampa
Riviera Beach

○ negro population exceeds 15%
✳ riot cities

% of total population
☐ 0-10 %
▨ 10-25 %
▩ 25-50 %
■ 50-84 %

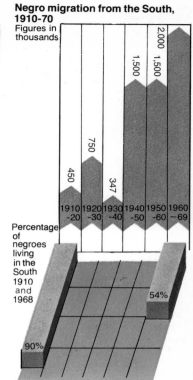

1910-20	1920-30	1930-40	1940-50	1950-60	1960-69
450	750	347	1,500	1,500	2,000

Percentage of negroes living in the South 1910 and 1968
90%
54%

From Civil Rights to Black Power

Civil rights are the rights that any citizen should be able to expect in a democratic country. They include the right to vote and to be treated fairly in law.

"Segregation" laws separated black and white citizens in the South. This is where the protest movement began. Negroes entered "white" restaurants and refused to use segregated buses.

Churches supported the movement. A minister from Alabama, Martin Luther King, took the lead in fighting racialism with non-violent demonstrations and freedom marches. White liberals also gave support. When King was arrested, Kennedy denounced the act and Negroes felt that they had friends in the highest places.

From 1962, Negroes began to get on voting registers in the South. Yet northern Negroes were impatient. They had had civil rights for years and they wanted more — escape from the ghettos (slums) and fair chances of employment.

Some rejected the idea of trying to become like white citizens. They looked instead towards Africa and the Muslim faith. Leaders like Malcolm X called for a bloodless revolution. Negroes increasingly supported the militant Black Power movement of Eldridge Cleaver and

Left: Martin Luther King's supporters display his picture after his death in Memphis in 1968.
Above: two American athletes, medal-winners at the 1968 Olympic Games, raise clenched fists in the Black Power salute.

Stokeley Carmichael.

In 1968, after Martin Luther King's assassination, America was convulsed by Negro riots in 125 cities. The policy of non-violence seemed to be dead.

However, King's successor, Ralph Abernathy, carried on his ideas. He sought to improve his people's lot by peaceful means and founded the Poor People's Campaign for all of America's unprivileged groups.

The Challenge of the Sea

More than two-thirds of the world's surface consists of ocean. Most of it is still unexplored and teeming with food in the form of fish, plankton and marine vegetation. These may one day feed the world's hungry millions.

While aircraft have almost completely replaced the great ocean-going liners for passenger transport, world trade still depends heavily upon shipping. Ocean trade routes are busier than ever before. Britain's Mercantile Marine, for instance, is bigger today in its over-all tonnage than in 1939. Despite cars and aircraft, half of Britain's food, a third of her fuel and 90 per cent of her raw materials must still come by sea. A dramatic change in ocean transport may come with the building of giant nuclear-powered cargo-carrying submarines, designed to carry great bulks of grain, oil and iron-ore. These ships would be faster than surface vessels. They would be immune from bad weather and less easily attacked in time of war.

20th century naval warfare has seen the passing of the battleship. Her one-time supremacy is now shared by nuclear-powered aircraft-carriers and submarines.

Below: British K-class submarine of World War One. The Germans began the first submarine campaign, attacking Allied shipping in 1915. They achieved spectacular success until checked by the convoy system.

In World War Two, submarines hunted in packs. The snorkel device enabled them to recharge batteries without surfacing. Modern nuclear-powered submarines can remain submerged almost indefinitely.

Above: Mountbatten hovercraft, 1968. It is able to carry 250 passengers. Christopher Cockerell invented the Hovercraft early in the 1950's. He discovered that a boat need not churn through the water, but could move above it, hovering on a "cushion" of air.

TITANIC SUNK.

TERRIBLE LOSS OF LIFE FEARED.

COLLISION WITH AN ICEBERG.

In April 1912, the liner *Titan* struck an iceberg and sank with the loss of 1,513 lives. The disaster led to new safety regulations at sea and better radio communication.

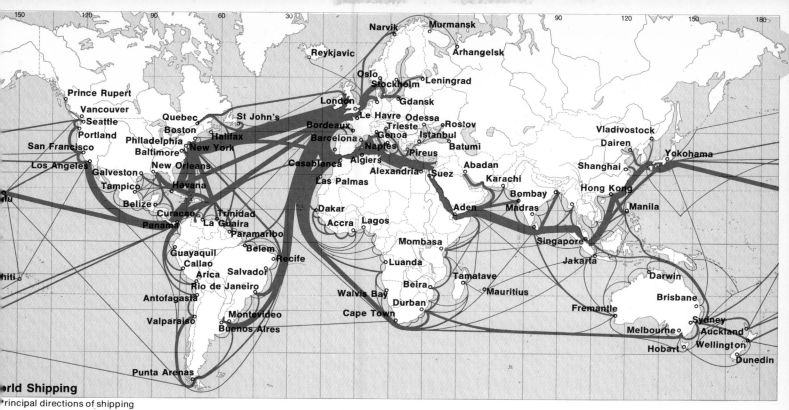

World Shipping

Principal directions of shipping
(The thickness of the lines is proportional to the frequency and to the total tonnage of traffic)

Above: the world's main shipping routes. They are heaviest in the North Atlantic. Closure of the Suez Canal (1967) has increased use of the South Africa route.

Below: Underwater house, Beehive Bay, off the coast of the U.S. ''Aquanauts'' can live here for long periods. Are underwater cities a possibility for the future?

Aviation

The Wright brothers made the first successful powered flight in 1903. It lasted twelve seconds but, within ten years, aeroplanes were making cross-country flights and military experts had begun to develop a new weapon.

Design and performance improved rapidly during World War One, while the inter-war years saw the pioneering of civil air-routes. The first flights across the Atlantic and the Pacific were made, and flyers reached out to India, South Africa, Australia and South America. This was the period of air heroes and heroines. It was also the era of flying-boats and ill-fated airships, vast gas-filled balloons.

War again brought tremendous technical advances which led, from 1946, to the development of an international industry. Aviation now provides travel for millions of passengers, air-freight services, and facilities for sport, rescue and exploration. Jumbo jets and supersonic speeds have added a new dimension to air travel. But aircraft have proved a mixed blessing; they pollute the atmosphere, require large areas of land near cities and produce intolerable noise levels.

Above: The Short reconnaissance seaplane of World War One. It was driven by a 150 h.p. engine and could travel at 61 m.p.h. (98 k.p.h.).

Below: Lockheed Shooting Star, a jet fighter. It was developed during World War Two, when jets first appeared. Its top speed was 558 m.p.h. (898 k.p.h.).

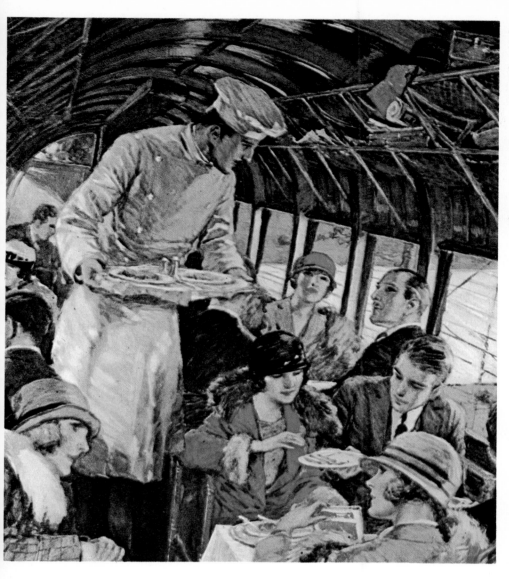

Charles Lindbergh, the first man to fly the Atlantic solo (1927). Pilots like Alan Cobham, Charles Kingsford-Smith, Wiley Post, Jean Batten and Amy Johnson became world-famous during the inter-war years.

Left: Air-travel on the London—Paris route, 1926. Handley-Page Transport Ltd. started this service in 1919, using converted bombers. These were later replaced by De Havilland biplanes carrying 22 passengers.

Below: Concorde, the Franco-British delta-wing machine, powered by four turbo-jets. It can carry over 100 passengers at supersonic speeds of up to 1,354 m.p.h. (2,179 k.p.h.).
   Supersonic flight has disadvantages; high fuel consumption and noise.

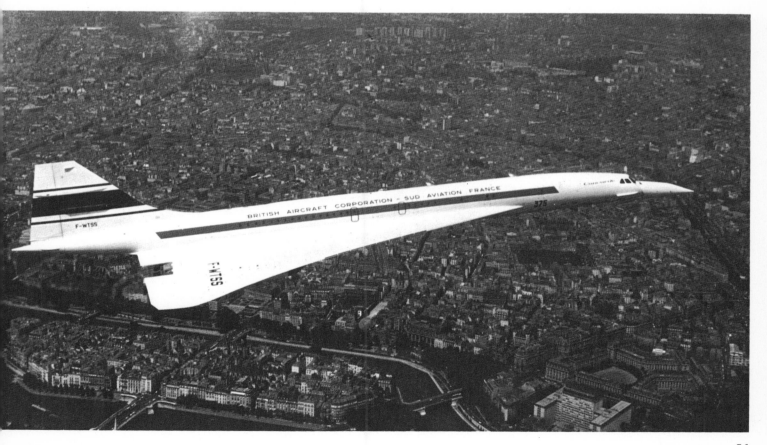

Agriculture

About 150 years ago, 80 per cent of the world's population had to work on the land. Today, in the United States, a mere six per cent of the population can produce enough food to feed that country and millions abroad.

A revolution in farm production has been brought about by the use of machinery, with the tractor as maid-of-all-work. Cheap electricity has made possible such devices as mechanical milking and automatic feeding of livestock. But the most striking development in modern farming has been the success of modern research into soils, cereals, livestock, grasses, fertilizers and pesticides. Grains, particularly dwarf wheat and hybrid maize, have been bred to give larger yields in drier, cooler conditions. Scientific breeding produces better animals. Nitrogenous fertilizers are obtained from the air. Disease and pests are controlled by spraying.

Some methods are harmful, however. "Factory farming", especially large-scale production of poultry, pigs and calves can be cruel. The danger of soil-erosion through over-cultivation is well-known in America and Australia.

Threshing Wheat by Thomas Benton, 1939, when steam tractors were still used to power farm machinery and horses pulled the harvest waggons. The artist expresses the spirit of agriculture allied to industry.

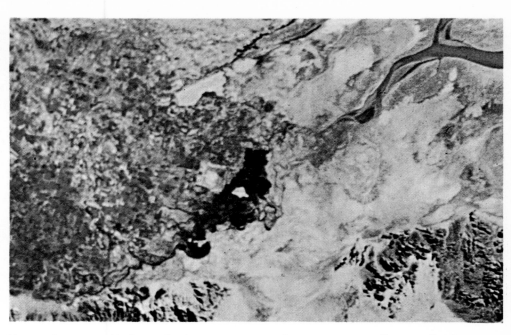

A farmer pours an insecticide into a spraying-machine on his tractor. The long-term effects of pesticides require constant research.

How science can help agriculture: this infra-red photograph shows up healthy (red) and diseased (blue) trees. Aerial surveys are still being made to prepare soil maps for large parts of the world. Modern agriculture calls on the services of biochemists and microbiologists.

An Electric World

Generating stations, electric lighting, electric trams and underground trains were in use by 1900. But electricity has only been used as the main source of domestic and industrial power in this century. In Britain, the Central Electricity Board was set up in 1926. It replaced the scores of small power stations with large stations sited close to their fuel supplies, and constructed a national network of transmission lines. Charles Parsons' invention of the steam turbine so increased output that by 1939, Britain had 58 turbo-generators and the country's electrical supply had increased nearly seven times since 1920. Even so, it was not until after World War Two that electricity became available to almost every home, workshop and factory.

The benefits are enormous. Clean, economical and adaptable, electricity provides industry with power for every kind of process, from lifting gear to computers. On the railways, it has replaced steam; in communications, it gives us telephones, radio, cinema and television; it has transformed our homes. Yet problems arise when a whole city may depend on a single power station for so much of its lighting, heating and entertainment.

Carrion Company electric cooker of 1912.

Electric washing machine, 1920's, with hand-wringer.

Electricity in the Home

The first benefit to the housewife was that she was now able to switch on the light, rather than have to strike matches for gas and oil-lamps which needed cleaning and constant attention.

Electric cookers made their appearance before 1914, but, like vacuum cleaners and washing machines, did not come into widespread use until about the 1950's. Many homes are now heated electrically or use an electric pump for central heating. Gadgets of all kinds are commonplace, from mixers, toothbrushes and shavers to power drills.

The Source of Electricity

Electricity can be obtained from the chemical energy in coal, gas or oil. It can also be obtained from the energy of moving water or from atomic energy. Generators convert these energy sources into electricity.

Many generators are driven by steam turbines. These are rotary engines whose blades are turned by powerful steam jets. In most power stations, burning coal heats water to produce the steam. That is why homes and industry still rely heavily on coal.

In countries with waterfalls or rivers on which dams can be built, generators are driven by the power of the water. This is called "hydro-electric" power.

Since the 1950's, numbers of atomic power stations have been built to harness nuclear energy. So far, however, their performance has been disappointing.

Electricity is uneconomical and inconvenient to store in large quantities. Accidents, strikes or lack of fuel can plunge large areas into darkness and bring industry to a standstill.

Refrigerator of about 1937. Earlier refrigerators simply used ice blocks. Today, they use a liquid refrigerant with an electric motor to work the condenser in the base.

Below: advertising signs in New York. Mercury vapour and sodium lamps came into use in the 1930's for street lighting, while neon-filled tubes provided brilliant colours.

Sport and Leisure

The main feature of sport in the 20th century has been its ever-increasing professionalism. Sport is organized as a multi-million industry for mass audiences. With intensive training, man has shown an astonishing capacity for record-breaking. Before Roger Bannister ran a mile in four minutes in 1953, it had seemed an impossible feat. Today, it is almost commonplace. The status of sportsmen has risen. 70 years ago, leading boxers, jockeys and footballers were lowly craftsmen. Today, they are highly paid stars, some of them millionaires. Organized sport used to occur only in a few rich nations; Britain, France and the U.S. It is now international. A footballer from Brazil, or an athlete from Kenya may prove himself the best in the world.

Edwardian bathing-styles at a time when sea-bathing was something of a novelty and sun-bathing had hardly been thought of. Competitive swimming is a fairly new sport. It is one in which champions are usually teenagers.

Right: Henry Cotton, one of the few British golfers to challenge the American superiority between the wars. He won the Open in 1934, 1937 and 1948. Golf is probably the world's fastest-growing sport today.

Right: Maureen Gardener training for the 1948 Olympics. Events for women were not included in the Games until 1928. Since then, some splendid women athletes have emerged.

Women take less part in professional sport, though tennis and golf are two exceptions. For physical reasons, their performances do not often match men's. In show-jumping and other kinds of riding, however, they fully hold their own.

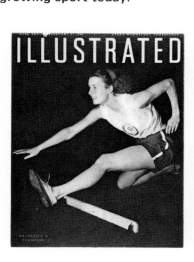

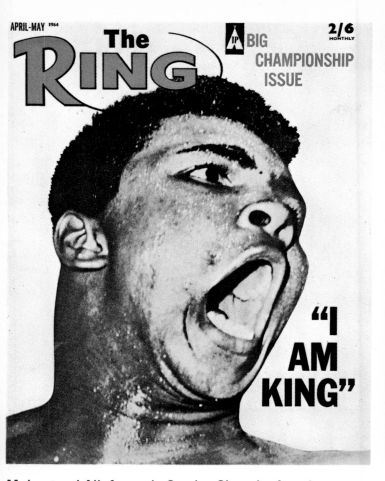

APRIL-MAY 1964

The RING

IP

2/6 MONTHLY

BIG CHAMPIONSHIP ISSUE

"I AM KING"

Mohammed Ali, formerly Cassius Clay, the American boxer who is a rich professional sports star.

TOKYO 1964

XVIII
OLYMPIC GAMES
OCT. 10-24

Japanese poster for the 1964 Olympic Games at Tokyo. Olympic athletes are all amateurs.

England's football team after winning the World Cup in 1966. Bobby Charlton holds the cup aloft.

International Competitions: The Olympics

Modern athletics had their beginnings in the 1896 Olympic Games in Athens, when 300 athletes from only 12 nations took part. The Games followed at four-year intervals. By 1964, at Tokyo, over 5,700 competitors from 94 nations contested 20 sports. At Munich, in 1972, the American swimmer Mark Spitz won the record number of seven gold medals.

Winter Olympics, for sports like ski-ing and skating, have been held at snow resorts like St Moritz and Grenoble since 1924.

The World Cup

Association football probably draws more spectators and arouses more enthusiasm throughout the world than any other sport. The World Cup Competition is staged every four years. 16 teams take part in the final round, having reached the finals after eliminating matches.

Uruguay won the first competition in 1930. Post-war winners have been: Uruguay (1950), West Germany (1954), Brazil (1958), Brazil (1962), England (1966) and Brazil (1970). England's sole victory in the game she originated came when she beat West Germany 4-2 at Wembley.

57

The Roads to Freedom

Since 1945, almost all the European colonial empires have dissolved. France fought in vain to keep Indo-China and Algeria. Holland had to yield to Indonesia's nationalist movement. Belgium quit the Congo in such haste that the country was soon involved in civil war. The same might be said of the British departure from India; the independence granted in 1947 was followed by savage disorder.

Nevertheless, once India had been granted self-government, there was no case for delaying it elsewhere. Only racial antagonism (as in Kenya and Cyprus), Communist terrorism (in Malaya) or economic weakness caused special difficulties. After 1947 the new African states came into existence, most of the West Indies became free and so did scattered dependencies, like Aden, Fiji and Tonga.

Independence was usually achieved with smoothness and goodwill, but the removal of imperial government sometimes caused bitter rivalries to come to the surface. There has been civil war in Nigeria and upheavals and one-party governments in a number of other new states.

The partition of India

- Predominantly Muslim
- Predominantly Hindu
- Predominantly Buddhist
- ▬ ▬ Boundaries between India and Pakistan after independence, 15th August 1947
- ── Provincial and state boundaries before partition

N.W. FRONTIER PROVINCE · KASHMIR Disputed by India and Pakistan · Lahore · Amritsar · PUNJAB · WEST PAKISTAN · BALUCHISTAN · Delhi · UNITED PROVINCES · SIKKIM · SIND · RAJPUTANA · Karachi · ASSAM · STATES OF WESTERN INDIA · Allahabad · BIHAR · BENGAL · Dacca · Calcutta · CENTRAL INDIA · CENTRAL PROVINCES · EAST PAKISTAN (now BANGLADESH) · Bombay · HYDERABAD · EASTERN STATES · BOMBAY · ORISSA · GOA · MADRAS · MYSORE · TRAVANCORE

Map of India showing distribution of Hindu and Muslim populations. When India gained independence, two states came into existence, India and Pakistan (itself divided into two parts). Religious rivalry was deep-seated, and massacres occurred, especially in the Punjab.

War broke out between India and Pakistan over Kashmir in 1965. It broke out again in 1971. Pakistan was heavily defeated, and East Pakistan became a new, independent state called Bangladesh.

Example of *apartheid*: white women rest on a seat marked, in English and Afrikaans, "Europeans Only".

Apartheid

In South Africa, the ruling class comprises less than four million white persons of European stock. There are about 15 million Africans and two million "coloureds".

Since 1948, the Nationalist Party has adopted the policy called *apartheid* ("separateness"). This provides separate housing and education for Africans. They are not allowed the same civil rights as whites, nor a real share in government.

Apartheid arouses hostility in the new African states and in the United Nations, but South Africa is unmoved by criticism. In 1961 she left the Commonwealth.

Prime Minister Julius Nyerere in Tanganyika's independence celebrations. With only a tiny white population, there were few problems in granting independence and Tanganyika has proved itself one of the most stable African countries. It took the name Tanzania in 1964.

"Boss" Lilford, farmer and supporter of the Rhodesian Front. Southern Rhodesia (population four million, of whom some 200,000 are white) was a self-governing colony from 1923.

It did not gain independence because Britain wanted it granted on terms acceptable to *all* Rhodesians

and very few Africans had a vote.

The 1961 Constitution, meant to lead to majority rule, was opposed by the Rhodesian Front. It's leader, Ian Smith, declared Rhodesia independent in 1965. Despite British and African opposition, Rhodesia has survived with help from South Africa.

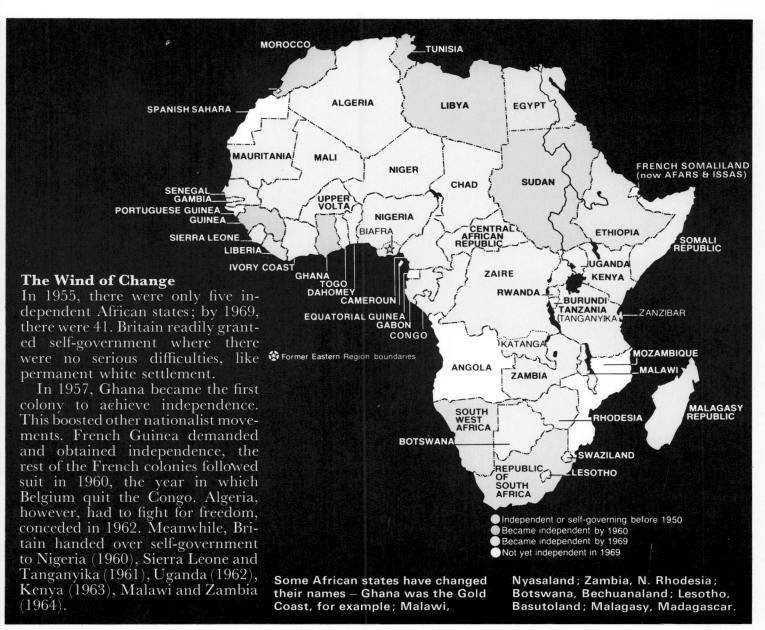

The Wind of Change

In 1955, there were only five independent African states; by 1969, there were 41. Britain readily granted self-government where there were no serious difficulties, like permanent white settlement.

In 1957, Ghana became the first colony to achieve independence. This boosted other nationalist movements. French Guinea demanded and obtained independence, the rest of the French colonies followed suit in 1960, the year in which Belgium quit the Congo. Algeria, however, had to fight for freedom, conceded in 1962. Meanwhile, Britain handed over self-government to Nigeria (1960), Sierra Leone and Tanganyika (1961), Uganda (1962), Kenya (1963), Malawi and Zambia (1964).

Map labels: MOROCCO, TUNISIA, SPANISH SAHARA, ALGERIA, LIBYA, EGYPT, MAURITANIA, MALI, NIGER, CHAD, SUDAN, FRENCH SOMALILAND (now AFARS & ISSAS), SENEGAL, GAMBIA, PORTUGUESE GUINEA, GUINEA, UPPER VOLTA, NIGERIA, CENTRAL AFRICAN REPUBLIC, ETHIOPIA, SOMALI REPUBLIC, SIERRA LEONE, LIBERIA, BIAFRA, IVORY COAST, GHANA, TOGO, DAHOMEY, CAMEROUN, UGANDA, ZAIRE, KENYA, RWANDA, BURUNDI, EQUATORIAL GUINEA, GABON, CONGO, TANZANIA (TANGANYIKA), ZANZIBAR, KATANGA, MOZAMBIQUE, MALAWI, ANGOLA, ZAMBIA, SOUTH WEST AFRICA, RHODESIA, MALAGASY REPUBLIC, BOTSWANA, SWAZILAND, REPUBLIC OF SOUTH AFRICA, LESOTHO

✪ Former Eastern Region boundaries

◯ Independent or self-governing before 1950
◯ Became independent by 1960
◯ Became independent by 1969
◯ Not yet independent in 1969

Some African states have changed their names – Ghana was the Gold Coast, for example; Malawi, Nyasaland; Zambia, N. Rhodesia; Botswana, Bechuanaland; Lesotho, Basutoland; Malagasy, Madagascar.

The British Common- wealth

Between 1947 and 1973, more than 30 former British colonies won their independence. Many might have decided to break all connections with Britain. Yet, almost all chose to join the Commonwealth. Today, it numbers 32 states whose populations make up one quarter of the world's people.

They have only two things in common. All are lands which the British once administered, and so still feel the influence of British traditions in fields as different as sport, language and law. All, even the republics, regard the Queen as a symbol of their association.

The Commonwealth is an association of independent nations. It has no fixed rules, it imposes no compulsion, and it is flexible enough to include members with widely differing views. There are, of course, solid reasons of trade and finance to keep the partnership going. There have been serious differences over, for example, the Suez crisis, the Common Market, and Rhodesia. But the essence of the Commonwealth is a belief in freedom and a willingness to discuss issues in a spirit of tolerance and goodwill.

Above: tribesmen at Kano in Northern Nigeria. In some countries, tribal rivalries, which had remained quiet under British rule, have emerged.

In Nigeria, there were three distinct regions and numerous tribes with their own loyalties, different languages and ways of life.

In 1967, the Eastern region (whose dominant tribe was the Ibo people) declared itself an independent state called Biafra. It was defeated by the Nigerian federal armies in a tragic civil war that lasted until January 1970.

Many races

The population of the Commonwealth now exceeds 860 million. What was a mainly British and Christian association has changed into one that is largely Asian and African, of Hindu, Muslim and Buddhist religion.

The populations of the new African nations number about 120 million—more than the total of the original members, Britain, Canada, Australia and New Zealand. India's population alone is about 548 million.

As an international association, the Commonwealth can claim to set an example to the world in the co-operation of many races.

Mr Menzies of Australia, Mrs Bandaranaike of Ceylon (Sri Lanka) and President Nkrumah of Ghana at the Commonwealth Conference, 1964.

Pandit Nehru, India's first Prime Minister, smeared with powder during a Hindu festival. He was educated in England and admired British culture and institutions. Nevertheless, like Gandhi, he respected India's ancient traditions.

Young cricketers in Trinidad. The British influence has been long-lasting. Many Commonwealth leaders receive their education in England, and the English language, styles of dress and sports may be found all over the world. The Commonwealth Games, rugby football, tennis, golf and, above all, cricket form enduring links between member countries.

61

The New Britain

Post-war Britain has undergone a social transformation. The 1945 Labour Government brought the Welfare State into being, to protect every citizen from illness, accident, unemployment and the disabilities of old age. Later governments extended these benefits. With full employment, and mass production, Britain, by 1970, was prosperous. People generally were better fed, better housed and better clothed; they spent more money and enjoyed more leisure than ever before. Yet this "affluent society" was precarious. Britain depended upon selling goods abroad where competition was fierce. Prices and wages rose too fast at home, creating inflation. Industrial unrest was ever-present and strike action so frequent that it was known to continentals as "the English disease". The nation that had endured and achieved so much seemed unable to bridge its divisions and solve its economic problems.

As her Empire dissolved, Britain had to decide on her new place in the world. The Suez crisis dented Britain's prestige as a world power, and she had to swallow her pride again when France refused her entry into the Common Market.

The Common Market

The European Economic Community, or Common Market, is an association designed to bring economic and, eventually, political union to Europe. It was founded in 1957 at the Treaty of Rome, by France, West Germany, Italy, Belgium, the Netherlands and Luxembourg.

Britain stayed out. She feared that she would lose her independence, and her close ties with the U.S. and the Commonwealth. Instead, she joined the looser European Free Trade Association with Austria, Denmark, Portugal, Sweden, Norway and Switzerland.

The Common Market's progress was so dynamic, however, that in 1961, the Conservative Government decided to apply for entry. Edward Heath seemed to have concluded negotiations successfully, when De Gaulle demanded an end to the business. Agreement had to be unanimous, so the French decision overruled the other members.

In 1965, the Labour Government met with a similar rebuff and it was not until 1972 that Heath took Britain "into Europe". Yet, by this time, there was strong opposition to entry in Britain itself. It remains to be seen whether the long-expected benefits will come.

Edward Heath on the cover of a German magazine, 1961.

Immigrant boys on their way to school in England. The arrival of about one million Commonwealth immigrants has caused problems in housing and employment, and gives rise to prejudice. The Race Relations Act (1968) made racial discrimination illegal.

Foxhunting, a leisure activity traditionally reserved for the upper classes, though it is now enjoyed by others too. The gulf between rich and poor has narrowed, but getting some jobs and types of education is still much easier for those who are already well-off.

Bingo, a popular activity in post-war Britain. People have more money for spending — and gambling; hence the crazes for bingo and betting shops. Yet, like pubs and holiday camps, bingo halls also satisfy people's desire to enjoy themselves as a group. They give a feeling of community.

Jimi Hendrix, wizard of the electric guitar, performs at the Marquee Club in London. For a brief period in the 1960's, Britain took over from America as the centre of fashion and popular music. Notice the military jacket; at a time when Britain had broken with her imperial past, it became fashionable to wear clothes that reflected the trappings of the Empire.

The Queen and Prince Charles at the Prince of Wales' investiture, Caernarvon Castle, 1969. The occasion caused some protest among Welsh Nationalists, who, like Scottish Nationalists, have demanded a greater degree of self-government since the 1960's. The Monarchy itself has adapted well to the changing world. There is practically no republicanism in Britain.

Ireland Divided

Asquith introduced a Bill to give Ireland its independence (Home Rule) in 1912, but Protestants in Ulster bitterly opposed the idea. War in 1914 put Home Rule into cold storage, though Irish nationalists remained active; Padraic Pearse led a revolt, the Easter Rising, in Dublin in 1916. It was easily suppressed, but, by executing its leaders, the British Government infuriated Irish patriots. Sinn Fein, the nationalist party, won a majority in the 1918 election. It formed an Irish parliament and declared a republic. Guerrilla warfare followed until, in 1921, the Treaty of Ireland was signed. Southern Ireland became the Irish Free State, separate from six counties of Ulster which formed Northern Ireland.

De Valera was the President of the Irish Free State (Eire from 1937). He wanted complete independence. Eire did not enter World War Two and left the Commonwealth in 1949. But the problem of Ulster remained. Was it to remain separate from Eire for ever? Could the hostility between Catholics and Protestants give way to trust and co-operation? What were the hopes for a united Ireland?

To Ulster Protestants, Home Rule meant "Rome Rule"—rule by the Catholic Church. They were ready to fight rather than be ruled by Catholics in Dublin. Bonar Law, leader of the English Conservatives, encouraged them. Edward Carson and James Craig took the lead in organizing resistance.

In 1913, the Ulster Volunteer Force, 100,000 strong, began military training. In the South, the Catholics formed the Irish Nationalist Volunteers. Only the outbreak of war in Europe prevented civil war in Ireland.

Ulster Volunteers in training, 1914.

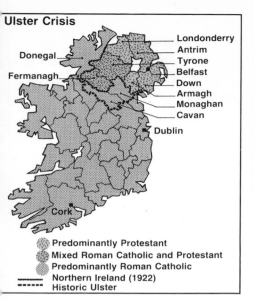

Ulster Crisis

Donegal

Fermanagh

Londonderry
Antrim
Tyrone
Belfast
Down
Armagh
Monaghan
Cavan

Dublin

Cork

Predominantly Protestant
Mixed Roman Catholic and Protestant
Predominantly Roman Catholic
Northern Ireland (1922)
Historic Ulster

Partition of Ireland, 1921. Four largely Protestant counties — Londonderry, Antrim, Down and Armagh — with Tyrone and Fermanagh, form Northern Ireland, part of the U.K.

Royal Ulster Constabulary try to keep order during a civil rights march in January, 1969.

Hopes that a divided Ireland might one day be united alarmed Protestants and made Catholics impatient. A civil rights movement attacked discrimination against the Catholic minority in Ulster.

Demonstrations for equal opportunities in jobs, housing and elections were met with violence. The police were accused of favouring the Protestants. Barricades were set up, petrol bombs and snipers appeared. The Northern Ireland Government asked for British troops to restore order.

British troops in Londonderry; called in for guard duty, they were reviled and attacked by both sides.

The Troubles Today

When violence erupted in 1968, old fears and hatreds came to the surface in Ulster. A branch of the I.R.A. (Irish Republican Army), the "Provisionals", attacked army units and carried on a campaign of bombing and murder. Separate Catholic and Protestant areas had to be set up, and extreme Protestant groups joined in the violence.

Parliamentary government became impossible. In 1972, direct rule from Westminster was introduced. By 1974, hopes rested on a new Assembly and the setting up of a Council of Ireland. Extremists, however, remained implacable.

An Irish family in Birmingham. Emigration to England has long been a way of escaping unemployment and bad housing in Ireland.

65

Australia and New Zealand

In both world wars, Australia and New Zealand came readily to Britain's aid, for there were many links of race, sentiment, trade and sport between these Dominions and the "mother country". Since World War Two, they have advanced rapidly. Both are stable, prosperous countries, attractive to immigrants, proud of their achievements and confident of the future. The people are overwhelmingly European in origin, and possess high levels of education and technical skill. More and more live in towns, and in Australia, work in industry. The populations are small—Australia has about 13 million and New Zealand 3 million inhabitants. Yet both countries play a large part in international affairs. Standards of living are among the highest in the world.

They have come to look beyond the Commonwealth for defence and trade. They are Pacific countries; when the last war showed that Britain could no longer guarantee their security, they looked toward the United States. New Zealand still trades principally with Britain, but Australia now does more business with America, Japan and South-East Asia.

The "outback" of the Northern Territory in Australia. The outback has played a great part in creating the Australian Legend; although most Australians now live in cities, they are deeply aware of their country's enormous size, and of the vast empty areas of "bush". This makes them feel that they are frontiersmen; manly, impatient of affectation and authority, hospitable and loyal to their mates.

Trade and Industry

New Zealand's prosperity rests chiefly on agriculture. Although she has coal and gas, mineral wealth is small, apart from great potential resources of iron ore.

Australia, on the other hand, has become increasingly industrialized. The country possesses coal, iron ore, copper, lead, gold, nickel, zinc, tin and silver. Agriculture, aided by water conservation schemes, remains important. To solve her labour shortage, Australia now welcomes immigrants from southern and eastern Europe.

Wool auctioneer in New Zealand whose main products are mutton, lamb, wool, dairy produce, beef and grain.

Left: aerial view of Sydney, whose skyscrapers contrast strongly with the outback. Like Melbourne, Sydney throbs with vitality. Its new Opera House (above) is one of the world's most startling and original buildings.

Surfing: Australians have a passion for outdoor life and sports.

Canadian Colossus

Canada ranks among the world's leading half dozen industrial and trading nations. She enjoys a standard of living second only, perhaps, to that of the United States. Her colossal development since 1918 has been due to cheap hydro-electric power, the discovery of huge mineral resources, vast forests and rapid industrialization. Canada is the world's greatest producer of nickel and zinc, and ranks second in silver, sulphur, molybdenum and uranium. In addition, she possesses petroleum, iron ore, gold, lead and natural gas. Her older industries, agriculture and fishing continue to thrive.

Wealth on such a scale gives Canada a great influence in world affairs. Though linked closely with the United States, she pursues her own, generally neutral, policies. Living alongside such a rich and powerful neighbour, it is sometimes hard for Canadians to feel their own "personality" as a nation. They are North Americans, and the people of the United States are their closest cousins. Yet this very closeness allows them to criticize America and to resist being overwhelmed by the American influence.

An International Power

In World War One, Canada sent six divisions to France, where they earned a high reputation under General Currie. In World War Two, Canadian troops served in the famous Dieppe raid, in North Africa, Italy and Normandy, and played a big part in the liberation of Belgium and Holland.

Since 1945, Canada has maintained forces to serve with N.A.T.O. in Europe. She contributed a brigade to the Commonwealth Division in the Korean War, and contingents to various U.N. peace-keeping forces, as in the Middle East after Suez, in the Congo and in Cyprus.

Canadian troops at the Battle of Ypres, which began in July 1917. They fought superbly to capture Passchendaele ridge.

Left: EXPO '67, held in Canada to celebrate the Dominion's centenary.

General De Gaulle encourages the Quebec separatists, 1967.

The Problem of Quebec

From the 17th century, Canada's pioneers included French farmers and fur-trappers who settled in the province of Quebec.

Here, for generations, they resisted all efforts to merge their language and customs with the dominant Anglo-Saxon ones. Compared with the rest of the country, Quebec remained backward. It cut itself off and jealously guarded its rights.

Since 1960, the province has been transformed. The old, corrupt political system has been replaced by a vigorous and honest administration. Yet grievances and a feeling of separateness have, if anything, grown stronger still.

French-Canadians number $5\frac{1}{2}$ million. They complain that Quebec's economy is under English-Canadian control; they fear "Americanization" and the loss of their independent culture. Some declare that they are Canada's "white Negroes". A separatist movement has arisen, demanding that Quebec leaves the Confederation to become an independent state.

69

Medicine

A tremendous advance in the scientific investigation of diseases has led to a world-wide improvement in health. People now realize that good housing, sanitation and nutrition are of supreme importance. Tuberculosis, scourge of rich and poor alike in the 19th century, is in decline. In addition to this general awareness, we can now inoculate against diphtheria, whooping cough, smallpox and poliomyelitis. Sulphonamides, penicillin and other anti-biotics have all made infections much less deadly. Apart from the use of drugs to cure and prevent illness, pain-killing drugs also make it easier for sufferers from incurable diseases.

X-rays and chemical investigations of blood samples give doctors a deeper understanding of the body. In a modern operating theatre, the surgeon can perform operations, such as kidney transplants, that were formerly impossible.

Medical progress and campaigns to wipe out diseases like malaria, plague, typhus and cholera, have contributed to the world's rise in population. So, as disease is overcome, new problems of feeding and housing arise.

Sigmund Freud (1856–1939). He founded modern "psycho-analysis" (investigation and treatment of the human mind). He believed that our sexual impulses provide the key to our personality and behaviour from our earliest years.

Attitudes to mental health have changed. People of low or disturbed mentality are now treated with understanding and medical care. New drugs, behaviour therapy, even hypnosis, help these people to take their place in the world.

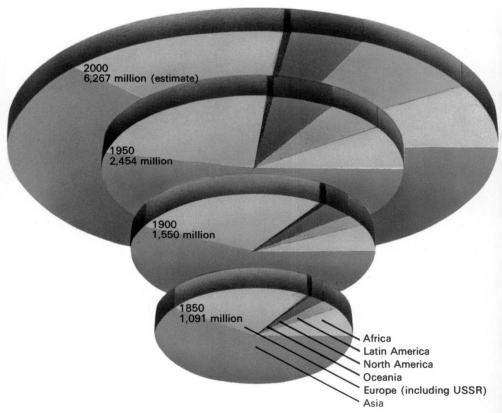

2000
6,267 million (estimate)

1950
2,454 million

1900
1,550 million

1850
1,091 million

Africa
Latin America
North America
Oceania
Europe (including USSR)
Asia

The Population Explosion

There are about 3,000 million people in the world today. Numbers are increasing so fast that the population is likely to double in the next 35 years.

Why has this happened? Food production has increased. Medicine, hygiene, and the care of mothers and babies have greatly improved. Healthy people are more fertile.

A rapidly increasing population gives rise to a host of problems.

Diagram illustrating the dramatic rise in the world's population since 1850. By the year 2000, it will probably have quadrupled in a century.

Food, housing and resources become scarce. Cities grow and the countryside shrinks. Over-crowding creates tensions and frustrations.

Birth-control to limit families has become acceptable in advanced countries, but so far, it has had little effect in areas like South America and Asia.

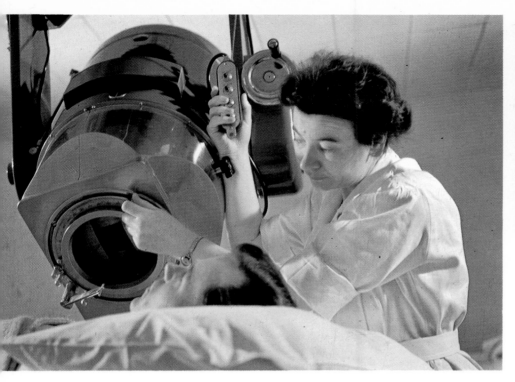

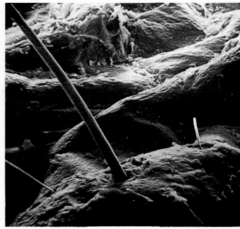

New scientific instruments increase knowledge of the body. Above: hairs on a human leg magnified 60 times by a scanning electron microscope.

Left: Gamma rays, produced by a radio-active material, are used to destroy cancer cells in the body. This is called "radio-therapy".

Sir Alexander Fleming, who discovered the "miracle drug", penicillin. He was working on antiseptics between the wars and accidentally discovered a mould, growing on a tray. It produced a liquid that killed off certain bacteria. These included the bacteria that caused pneumonia and diphtheria.

With the help of British and American scientists, penicillin was produced during World War Two. It came in time to save thousands who would otherwise have died from wounds and infections.

Left: Indian children bare their arms for inoculation. After World War One, the League of Nations began to tackle disease on an international scale. The World Health Organization was later set up, in 1948. Vaccination has made epidemics of deadly diseases much less common.

Our Crowded Cities

"Urbanization" means town-dwelling. It has grown at an even faster rate than the world's population. In 1900, there were only 160 towns with more than 100,000 inhabitants. By the 1960's, in the U.S. alone, over a third of the population lived in only 24 cities. Each had over a million inhabitants.

Massive problems arise when people congregate in such numbers. Cities consist of a city centre, a "suburban" fringe around the city, and a "conurban" sprawl—large areas which are neither town nor country. As a city spreads, the better-off tend to move into the suburbs and the centre decays. It may become a slum area, or be given over to business and administration. Millions may come to work in the centre, but few live there. Modern cities tend to look alike, with high-level blocks, stores and supermarkets, all built in similar materials. Yet civic pride still exists; fierce efforts are often made to maintain old buildings and communities. Some decayed centres have been successfully re-developed. Despite its problems, the city remains for many an exciting, attractive place, a centre of culture, entertainment and mystery.

An English pub. City life can be lonely, but the pub, like the French café, provides a meeting place which gives the feeling of a neighbourhood.

Below: shopping area of Levittown, Pennsylvania. The town has no centre. People need cars to get from a shopping to a working area.

Cities can be lively places. Yet the neighbourliness and traditions that are found in villages and small towns seldom exist.

City authorities have to deal with all kinds of problems that smaller communities do not face, or can handle more easily. Crime and vice are difficult to control in heavily-populated areas. Problems of health, water-supply, sewage and waste disposal become acute. Traffic con-

Urban congestion, old and new. Above: London Bridge, circa 1900. Right: New York today. Much of the centre is given over to commerce.

gestion builds up and car fumes, added to atmospheric pollution from factories, threaten public health. Overcrowding makes great difficulties for public transport. In some cities, like Los Angeles, public transport hardly exists.

Mass Society

Over the last 30 years, the advanced nations have attained astonishing material progress and wealth. Never before have so many people been so well off. The abundance of food and goods that we enjoy derives largely from mass production. This is a process that involves many workers, each making a part of a product, rather than a single worker making a product from beginning to end. It has become ever more efficient through modern technology, synthetic materials, work-study and the use of electronics and computer control. It is more profitable to turn out ten thousand cars (or dresses or washing machines) all identical, than numbers of different models, each requiring a separate design.

The car, dress or washing machine produced in large numbers can be sold more cheaply. Yet the public has less choice between goods. Advertising can persuade people that they want the goods that the giant corporations produce. It can suggest that a mass-produced drink or box of chocolates was made for one person alone—the customer. In short, mass production creates a mass society.

Break-time in the gardens of Cadbury's model factory at Bournville.

Conditions in modern factories have improved enormously since the days when workers toiled in "dark satanic mills". Employees are frequently provided with canteens, sports and social facilities. Some firms offer profit-sharing schemes. Nevertheless, mass production involves millions of workers in monotonous jobs. Few can experience the craftsman's pride in a finished object. Efforts are being made, as in the car industry in Sweden, to provide work which is more varied and satisfying.

Where it all started – adding bodies to Model 'T' Ford chassis in Detroit, over 60 years ago. Henry Ford pioneered mass production.
   Cars lend themselves well to the process. Car-workers are usually well paid, but the high-pressure work is very demanding.

Left: examining sales bargains in a London store in the 1950's. The rise of the ready-to-wear clothing industry has enabled people to be better and more hygienically dressed. Man-made materials, like nylon and terylene, are easy to produce on a mass scale.

Right: early advertisement tries to give Coca-Cola an air of fashion! Advertising has become a powerful, even sinister force. It creates a demand for things when there was none before. It influences the quality of newspapers, magazines, radio and television.

The Modern State

Democracy means government by the people. Democratic countries set great store upon freedom. Yet, in modern times, there has been a marked increase in the state's authority over ordinary citizens. Until this century, matters like employment, housing and education were left largely in private hands. Even in 1910, there was fierce opposition to Lloyd George's plans to introduce help for the sick and unemployed. Today, almost every human activity—work, play, eating, drinking, travelling, buying, selling, being born and dying—is hedged about by official regulations.

A civilized society has to have rules. Most people now accept the need for laws to protect the poor and the weak, and for some state control of business and industry. Yet a state needs officials, forms and paperwork to operate this control. This "bureaucracy" becomes powerful. People come to feel that, apart from voting occasionally, they have no say in government. Some take to unofficial protest, in America over Vietnam, in Britain over the atomic bomb, when they feel that the state is not representing them properly.

1910: one of the new Labour Exchanges set up to provide jobs.

A baby is born: it has been said of the National Health Service that it provides protection "from the womb to the tomb".

The Welfare State in Britain

A welfare state is one which guarantees certain basic rights and services to all citizens.

In Britain, it had its beginnings in the laws passed by the Liberal government of 1906. These brought in old-age pensions, labour exchanges and juvenile courts. There were laws covering wages and conditions in certain trades, and sickness and unemployment relief for some workers.

There was little progress during the 1920's and 1930's. During wartime, however, the government published a report, known as the Beveridge Plan. This recommended a thorough system of social insurance.

A Labour government took office, pledged to act on the report. By the National Insurance Act, 1946, almost everyone was protected against illness, accident and unemployment. Maternity allowances were added to the existing family allowances, and widows were given pensions.

The National Health Service was set up and provided medical, dental and eye treatment for everyone. A new programme improved hospitals and provided homes for the sick and aged.

The State has increasingly concerned itself with education. An Act of 1902 allowed local authorities to build state secondary schools for some children. The Fisher Act of 1918 abolished fees at elementary schools.

Secondary education for all began in 1944. The system of primary and secondary schools came in, with provision for further education. Since that time, there have been various alterations. The school leaving age has been raised to 16, and many comprehensive schools have been opened to unite the old grammar and secondary modern schools.

Protest against the Vietnam War: a student confronts U.S. Army bayonets with a flower. Unofficial protest demonstrations challenge the authority of the modern state.

DOWN WITH STATE CONTROL
Vote CONSERVATIVE

1964 Conservative poster stresses that Conservatives believe in private enterprise rather than state control. Yet, in office, they have not often abolished controls introduced by Labour.

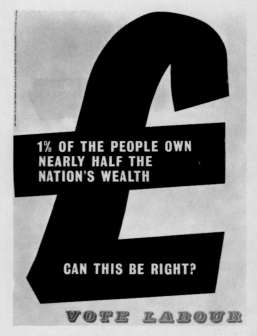

£

1% OF THE PEOPLE OWN NEARLY HALF THE NATION'S WEALTH

CAN THIS BE RIGHT?

VOTE LABOUR

Labour party poster. Labour traditionally stands for state control on behalf of the people. It believes that the state, rather than businessmen, should own and run some of the nation's industries.

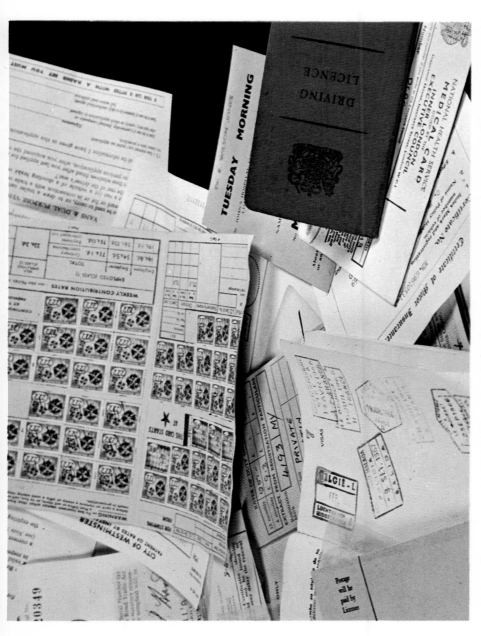

Some of the forms and documents that the modern state issues to its citizens. They include driving licence, Medical card, National Insurance card and rates demand. Unless a citizen fills in the right forms, he may find himself deprived of benefit or fined.

Fashion

Fashion tends to reflect society. This century's first decade was an extravagant era for the wealthy. Women's dress emphasized the female figure; men wore stiff collars, dark suits and hard hats, suitable for a time when men were the masters.

As women thought about freedom and the vote, they discarded corsets and wore loose gowns. Then, in order to do war work, they raised their skirts above the ankles and adopted military styles. In the 1920's, emancipated women wore shapeless tubular dresses, as if to show that they were not so different from men. They displayed their new freedom by baring their knees, arms, and, in the evenings, their backs. Curves and long skirts came back with the "New Look" of the 1940's, but in the 1960's, the hem-line rose again with the mini-skirt.

Today, fashion reflects the independence of youth. The freer styles also illustrate other changes; as houses become better heated, it is less important to be tightly buttoned, or to wear bulky underclothing. Yet old fashions can come back. "Teddy boys" aped Edwardian styles and, in the 1970's, young men are already copying the Teddy boys.

Edwardian lady at Ascot. Notice the large hat, elaborate sunshade and hobble skirt. The dress emphasizes the hips and bust. Invention of the brassiere in about 1913 added further emphasis. The cost of the outfit would have been high.

Right: "flapper" of 1924, with flat chest, shingled hair and lip-sticked mouth. Skirts were short and dresses loose. By 1930, they had become longer, with flares and flounces. Rayon and ready-to-wear clothes arrived.

The "New Look", whose feminine style was a reaction against wartime austerity. Nylon underwear had arrived.

Teddy boys in the 1950's wore "drain-pipe" trousers, long jackets, bootlace ties and slicked-back hair.

"Hippy" style, with long hair and flowing robes. The style suggests Eastern or gipsy women. It began as a reaction against high fashion and a money-making dress trade. Yet people found that selling beads, leather sandals and "way out" clothes could be very profitable.

Left: Mary Quant fashion of the 1960's. The cropped hair, short skirt and flat chest are remarkably similar to the flapper look of the 1920's. The high-necked straight shift reveals the legs, hiding the bust, waist and hips.

Modern Art

In no previous age have changes in the arts been so rapid, or old standards been so completely overthrown. Today, even educated people often greet a new painting, sculpture, play or novel with bewilderment. Why has art become so "difficult"?

New developments in society provide some clue. People used to believe that painters should copy what they saw; now photography can do that more accurately. Novelists, poets and playwrights used to be popular entertainers as well as artists; now films and television have captured the public. Artists today have to rely less on what others want than on their own ways of seeing the world. A painter may be obsessed by certain harmonies of colour and line. A novelist may explore the themes that haunt him. As they pursue their aims with greater dedication, it becomes difficult for the public to judge what is "good" and what is "bad". The artist's new position gives him greater freedom. A painter can stick fragments of newspaper onto his canvas, a novelist may use crude language. He need offer no set answer to the question "What is Art?" Like Picasso, he may reply, "What isn't?"

Improvisation No. 27 (1912) by Kandinsky, a Russian artist who worked mostly in Germany. He was the first to produce a wholly "abstract" painting – a picture that does not represent people or objects. He was more concerned with expressing his feelings through colour and line.

When people think, thoughts do not follow one another in an orderly way as most novelists pretend. James Joyce (above) developed a "stream of consciousness" style of writing. In *Ulysses*, he presented one day in the life of a Dublin Jew through the jumble of thoughts that pass through his characters' minds. The work is notoriously "difficult", yet it can be understood. Here, his hero is in a cemetery:

How many! All these here once walked round Dublin. Faithful departed. As you are now, so once were we. Besides how could you remember everybody? Eyes, walk, voice. Well, the voice, yes: gramophone. Have a gramophone in every grave or keep it in the house. After dinner on a Sunday. Put on old grandfather Kraahraark! Hello-hellohello amawfullyglad kraak awfullygladaseeragain hellohello amarawfkopthsth. Remind you of the voice like the photograph reminds you of the face. Otherwise you couldn't remember the face after fifteen years, say. For instance who? For instance some fellow that died when I was in Wisdom Hely's. Rtststr! A rattle of pebbles. Wait. Stop.*

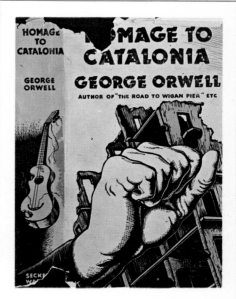

Pop art poster by Michael English. Pop artists do not often paint abstract pictures, but their work can be equally shocking. They depict subjects like soup cans which no-one would have thought "artistic" before.

Contrasts in the theatre: above, Ivor Novello and Gladys Cooper in *Iris*, a popular play of 1925. Cinema was already drawing audiences away from the theatre.

Below: *Endgame* by Samuel Beckett. The characters perform in dustbins. Beckett writes plays which have an atmosphere of bleak, meaningless despair. Virtually nothing happens.

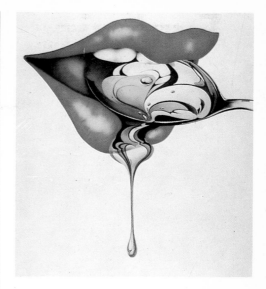

Not all writers and painters have withdrawn from society. The picture above shows the cover of George Orwell's book about the Spanish Civil War. He wrote other books tackling social and political themes, including *Animal Farm* which pointed to the dangers of Communism. Steinbeck, Caldwell and O'Neill wrote of poverty in America. Painters like Burra and Hopper showed scenes of everyday life. O'Casey described suffering and revolution in Ireland, and, more recently, James Baldwin has dealt with the plight of the American Negro.

*Extract from *Ulysses*, reproduced by kind permission of The Bodley Head Ltd., 1922.

Exploring Space

The Russians and Germans pioneered rocket technology in the 1930's. For most people, however, the space age began in 1957. In October of that year, an astonished world learnt that the Russians had launched a small satellite into space. It was called Sputnik I. A month later, Sputnik II carried a dog into orbit. America countered with Vanguard I, no bigger than a grapefruit, in 1958. The space race was on.

Progress was swift. In 1961, the Russian Yuri Gagarin became the first man to travel in space. He was closely followed by Shepard and Glenn of the United States. Only eight years later, the Americans achieved what still seems the greatest miracle of our age—the landing on the Moon.

Since then, there have been more lunar landings. Men have made long flights in orbiting laboratories—spacecraft from which it is possible to make detailed observations of the universe. Unmanned probes explore the planets and man may yet reach Mars and Venus. The space programmes will increase our knowledge of the universe. But they raise an awkward question—is the vast expenditure justified?

Above: the 200-inch (5,080 mm) reflector at Mount Palomar in California. It is one of the world's biggest optical telescopes.
Below: one of the world's largest radio telescopes at Parkes in New South Wales.

A "nebula", a cloud of gas and dust, ejected from a central star in our galaxy. Telescopes reveal the secrets of space. Astronomers use three main types: the "refractor", which has a lens or object-glass; the "reflector", in which light strikes a mirror and is reflected back to a second mirror and thence to the eye-piece; the "radio telescope", which collects radio waves coming from galaxies in outer space.

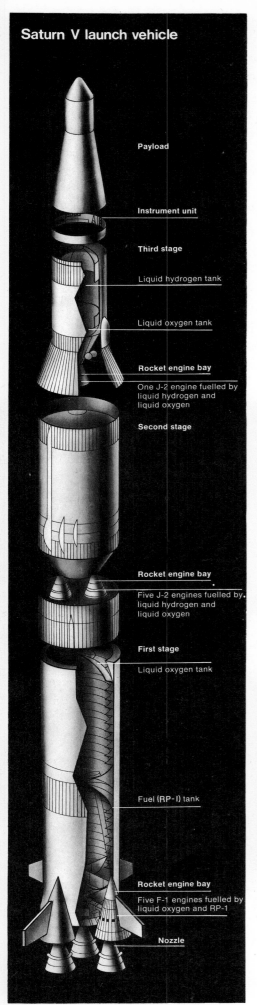

Saturn V launch vehicle

Payload

Instrument unit

Third stage

Liquid hydrogen tank

Liquid oxygen tank

Rocket engine bay

One J-2 engine fuelled by liquid hydrogen and liquid oxygen

Second stage

Rocket engine bay

Five J-2 engines fuelled by liquid hydrogen and liquid oxygen

First stage

Liquid oxygen tank

Fuel (RP-I) tank

Rocket engine bay

Five F-1 engines fuelled by liquid oxygen and RP-1

Nozzle

The Moon Landing

On 16 July 1969, after eight years of intensive research, America was ready to land the first men on the Moon's surface.

The Saturn V rocket achieved lift-off from the launch pad, thrusting the Apollo XI spaceship into its orbit around the Earth. The first and second stage rockets were jettisoned in the process.

Apollo XI contained Neil Armstrong, commander of the mission, Edwin Aldrin, lunar module pilot, and Michael Collins, command module pilot. The third stage rocket propelled the craft into its orbit around the moon and was jettisoned. Then, the lunar excursion module (L.E.M.), containing Armstrong and Aldrin, separated from the command module. Collins kept the command module in orbit.

L.E.M. braked and descended gently to land in the Sea of Tranquillity on the Moon. Six and a half hours later, Neil Armstrong climbed down the ladder. Watched by millions of breathless television viewers throughout the world, he set foot on the Moon's surface.

Aldrin followed. The two men set up scientific instruments and collected rock and dust samples.

To return to Earth, they took off in the ascent section of L.E.M. They rejoined Collins in the command module and, having jettisoned the ascent section, re-entered the Earth's atmosphere. The module descended by parachute into the Pacific Ocean.

Units of the U.S. Navy were waiting to pick up the astronauts. After eight days and a journey of half a million miles, they were only ten seconds late in making their splash-down.

Shortly after lift-off, the first stage is about to be jettisoned.

Collins orbits the command module 60 miles above the Moon.

Aldrin descends the ladder to join Armstrong on the Moon.

Left: diagram of Saturn V. The lunar and command modules were housed in the payload.

Aldrin photographed by Armstrong. He wears a space suit fitted with a life support system that includes oxygen to breathe, and water to cool his body. The controls are positioned on his chest.

Power and Pollution

Industrialized nations are using up vital coal and oil resources at a high rate. Scientists disagree about how long deposits will last, but it is certain that one day they must run out. The crisis could be temporary; since the 1950's, atomic power has been used to generate electricity, and it is calculated that there is enough uranium in the rocks and the sea to provide fission power for a million years. The sun's radiation may supply power in the future. New oil-fields may be discovered, as they have been in Britain's North Sea. It may become possible to produce oil synthetically from hydrogen in the sea and carbonic acid in the air. Until these possibilities are developed, however, oil-producing countries can demand high prices for their "black gold".

Our present sources of energy produce problems of waste disposal; slag-heaps and smoke from coal, sulphur di-oxide from oil-burning, fumes from motor vehicles. Oil pollutes the sea when it escapes, by accident or design, from tankers. There are already frightening accumulations of radio-active waste from nuclear power stations.

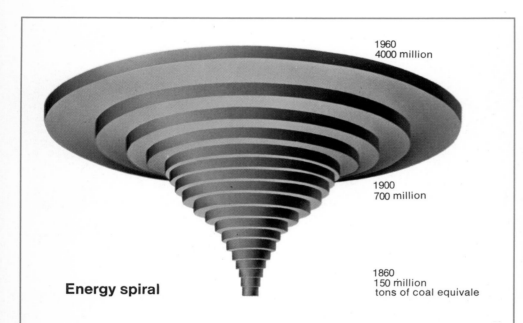

1960
4000 million

1900
700 million

1860
150 million
tons of coal equivale

Energy spiral

The Energy Crisis

The diagram above illustrates the tremendous growth of the world's energy production. The figures show the total amounts of energy, measured in tons of coal.

Some people predict that the reserves of natural gas and the major oil-fields will be exhausted by the end of the century. Yet new reserves may be discovered, and new energy sources may be developed. Atomic power is in its infancy. Scientists may produce synthetic fuels or harness the sun's energy.

Ford's experimental electric car. Petrol causes air pollution and becomes increasingly expensive. Efforts to produce an electric car are being intensified. The main requirement is a small battery that can be easily recharged. Such a car would be especially suitable for town travel.

Atomic Power

When atoms are split (see page 34), they emit neutrons, radiation, heat and energy. The neutrons may set off further fission, producing a chain reaction. This can be maintained and controlled in a nuclear "reactor". The energy from a reactor may be used in a power station to produce electricity.

The first commercial atomic power station was opened at Calder Hall, England, in 1956. Others followed, and most leading nations now produce some electricity by this means. But there are drawbacks. Stations are expensive, their efficiency has proved disappointing, and dangerous radio-active waste has to be disposed of.

The American scientist Fermi brings the world's first nuclear reactor to life, Chicago, 1942.

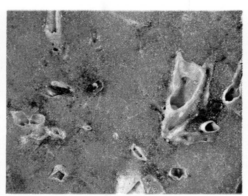

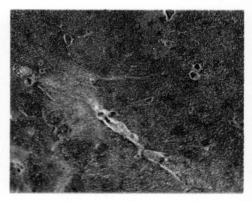

Above: healthy lung tissue of an 80-year old woman, a non-smoker. She came from Surrey which is a clean-air area. Right: lung-tissue from a 60-year old man, a smoker, from central London. Polluted air was considered to be the cause of blackening in this case.

Left: mass society's waste. It brings enormous problems of disposal, especially as plastic material is hard to destroy. Retrieval of waste, by re-pulping paper or re-using bottles, is possible, but it is often rejected as being too costly.

Disposal of suds at a Los Angeles sewage plant. Foam from household detergents can now be dealt with. "Industrial effluent" (chemical waste which is often pumped into rivers) remains a more serious problem.

Time Chart: the main events in world history

British Isles and Ireland

Britain has endured two gigantic wars, economic crises and industrial discontent. She has seen Ireland divided, her Empire dissolved and her position as a world power diminished. Yet there have been marked advances in living standards, social welfare and education.

Europe

Disrupted by war, Fascism and Communism, Europe remains divided. The West has, however, become united to some degree by the E.E.C.

1901
Death of Queen Victoria; accession of Edward VII (1901). Education Act (1902). Entente Cordiale with France. Liberal Government; Old Age Pensions. Asquith Prime Minister (1908), Lloyd George's "the People's Budget". Accession of George V (1911). Suffragette movement. Marconi transmitted radio signals. First electric trams. Dreadnought battleships, submarines, aeroplanes, cinemas. Cars and buses on roads. Boy Scouts founded.
Writers: Kipling, Conrad, Shaw, Wells, Bennett.
Music: Delius, Elgar. Science: Russell, Rutherford, Thompson.

Triple Alliance of Austria, Germany, Italy. Alexander of Serbia assassinated. Revolution in Russia (1905). Triple Entente of France, Britain, Russia. Austria annexed Bosnia. Anglo-German naval rivalry. Writers: Chekov, Mann, Gide. Science: Curie, Freud, Pavlov, Einstein. Music: Sibelius, Diaghilev. Art: Cézanne.

1911
National Insurance Act. Strikes. Unrest in Ulster; Curragh Mutiny. War declared on Germany (1914); Haig Commander in Chief. Conscription introduced. Easter Rebellion in Ireland (1916). Lloyd George Prime Minister (1916). "Khaki election" (1918); women over 30 given vote. Irish Civil War. Government of Ireland Act provided for partition. Fisher Education Act. Alcock and Brown flew Atlantic. Marconi Company started broadcasts. Council houses built. Influenza epidemic. London–Paris air services.
Writers: D. H. Lawrence, T. E. Lawrence, Brooke, Maugham. Music: Holst.

Agadir crisis. Italo-Turkish war. Balkan wars. Sarajevo; Austria attacked Serbia. World War One; Marne, Verdun, Jutland, Somme. Russian Revolution. Brest Litovsk. German offensive failed. Treaty of Versailles. Kapp Putsch. D'Annunzio seized Trieste. Russo-Polish war. Art: Dufy, Matisse. Music: Stravinsky. Writers: Proust, Kafka.

1921
Treaty of Ireland. Irish Free State founded; civil war. Lloyd George overthrown; Bonar Law Prime Minister (1922). Baldwin Prime Minister (1923). First Labour Government (1924); Macdonald Prime Minister. General Strike (1926); Trades Disputes Act. Imperial Conference defined Commonwealth. Votes for women at 21 (1928). Widespread unemployment, hunger marches.
First Austin 7. Imperial Airways formed. Baird demonstrated television. Fleming discovered penicillin. Whittle at work on jet engines.
Writers: Forster, Huxley, Eliot, Joyce. Theatre: Noel Coward.

Civil War in Russia. Rise of Mussolini in Italy. Inflation in Germany. France occupied Ruhr. Hitler's Munich Putsch. Death of Lenin. Stalin's Five Year Plan. Poland ruled by Pilsudski.
Theatre: Brecht. Cinema: Eisenstein. Art: Surrealism. Architecture: Bauhaus. Writers: Gide, Maurois.

1931
Financial crisis: National Government, Macdonald Prime Minister. Unemployment reached three million. British Union of Fascists formed. Baldwin Prime Minister (1935). Edward VIII abdicated. Churchill demanded re-armament. Chamberlain Prime Minister (1938). Munich crisis (1938). War declared on Germany (1939). Churchill Prime Minister (1940). Battle of Britain. Blitz.
Nuclear Physics in Cambridge. Radar. Art: Epstein, Moore, Sutherland.
Writers: Woolf, Auden, Greene. Music: Britten, Beecham.

The Depression. Rise of Nazism. Hitler German Chancellor. Stavisky scandal in France. Dollfuss murdered in Austria. Rhineland occupied. Spanish Civil War. Soviet purges. *Anschluss*. Munich crisis. Nazi-Soviet pact. Poland invaded. *Blitzkrieg* in Western Europe. The Arts: Picasso, Klee, Kandinsky. Writers: Brecht, Céline. Cinema: Riefenstahl.

1941
Air raids. Women conscripted. Meeting of Churchill and Roosevelt; Atlantic Charter. Beveridge Plan. Education Act (1944). D-Day invasion. Labour Government (1945); Attlee Prime Minister. Nationalization programme. National Health Service introduced. Economic austerity; fuel restrictions, devaluation of the pound. B.B.C. television resumed. Town and Country Planning Act. Nuclear reactor built at Harwell.
Writers: Hartley, Orwell, Bates. Art: Moore, Nash.
Music: Bliss, Britten.

Hitler master of Europe. Invasion of Russia; Stalingrad. Allied invasion of Italy. Bombing of Germany. Normandy landings. July Plot. Paris liberated. Russian advance. German collapse. Deaths of Hitler, Mussolini. Communist control of Eastern Europe. The Cold War. Marshall Aid. Berlin blockade. Writers: Anouilh, Ionesco, Sartre.

1951
Festival of Britain. Conservative Government; Churchill Prime Minister (1951). Accession of Elizabeth II (1952). British atomic bomb. Eden Prime Minister (1955). Suez crisis. Macmillan Prime Minister (1958). Increased prosperity. Britain joined E.F.T.A. Campaign for Nuclear Disarmament. "New Look" fashions, Teddy boys. New towns, schools and universities. Commonwealth immigration. Commercial television; "kitchen sink" drama. Writers: Amis, Churchill, Shute, Thomas. Art: Moore, Piper. Theatre: Rattigan, Osborne, Wesker.

Russia produced atomic bomb. N.A.T.O. set up. Warsaw pact between Communist states. Hungarian revolt crushed. Suez crisis. E.E.C. and E.F.T.A. founded. Kruschev Russian premier. De Gaulle in France. German economic recovery under Adenauer. First Russian Sputnik satellites. Cinema: Fellini. Writers: Pasternak. Sagan.

1961
Balance of payments crisis. U.S. supplied Polaris missiles. Common Market entry vetoed by France. Douglas-Home Prime Minister (1963). Labour Government; Wilson Prime Minister (1964). Coal mines closures. Pay freeze. Pound devalued. The Beatles. Mini-skirts. England won World Cup (football). *Queen Elizabeth II*'s maiden voyage. Concorde flew. Strife in Northern Ireland; troops engaged. Conservative Government; Heath Prime Minister (1970).
Theatre: Pinter, Stoppard. Art: Bacon, Hamilton.

De Gaulle withdrew from N.A.T.O. Berlin Wall. Gagarin first man in space. Nuclear Test Ban Treaty. Soviet spaceship reached Venus. Spain closed Gibraltar frontier. Military coup in Greece. Student revolt in France, unrest in Italy and Spain. Russia invaded Czechoslovakia. De Gaulle resigned; franc devalued.

Asia and Australia

Japan became a world power. Israel and Mao's China were born, India became independent. Korea and Vietnam were torn by war.

Anglo-Japanese alliance. Russo-Japanese war. China in ferment after Boxer Rising. Japan annexed Korea. Curzon's reforms in India. Muslim League founded; Morley-Minto reforms. Young Turks deposed Sultan. Commonwealth of Australia founded (1901). New Guinea acquired by Britain. New Zealand became a Dominion (1907).

Chinese revolution; Sun Yat-sen President. China angered by Versailles Treaty. Japan built a navy, declared war on Germany. George V's Durbar at Delhi (1911). India supported Britain at war. Home Rule campaign. Amritsar Massacre (1919). Government of India Act. Gandhi emerged. Anzac troops fought at Gallipoli.

Washington Conference insisted that the powers respect China's independence. Sun Yat-sen accepted Russian aid. Chiang Kai-shek set up Nanking Government, attacked Communists. Mao Tse-tung founded Red Army. Japan took Shantung. Kemal proclaimed Turkish Republic. Gandhi's civil disobedience campaign in India. Australia encouraged British immigrants.

Japan occupied Manchuria, set up puppet state, left League of Nations, made pact with Germany. Nationalists and Communists fought in China; the Long March. Japan attacked China. Government of India Act gave provincial self-government (1935). New Zealand: first Labour Government (1935).

Japan took South-East Asia. Hiroshima. Japan occupied by U.S. forces. China at war until 1949; People's Republic proclaimed. India and Pakistan independent (1947). Burma, Ceylon, Philippines, Indonesia gained independence. State of Israel (1948). Korean War (1950–53). War in Vietnam between French and Communist Vietminh.

India: Nehru Prime Minister, trade pact with Russia. Pakistan: premier assassinated, pact with U.S., military takeover. Malaya independent, Singapore self-governing. French defeated in Vietnam. Indonesia: Sukarno expelled the Dutch. China: pact with Russia, Tibet invaded. Israel attacked Egypt.

India: Goa occupied, border clashes with China. Japan: rapid economic recovery. China; dispute with Russia, tension with Britain over Hong Kong, exploded its own atomic bomb. Indonesia: Sukarno overthrown. Australia: naval pact with U.S. Six Day war between Egypt and Israel (1967). War in Vietnam: U.S. forces withdrawn.

Africa

Most of Africa has been freed from colonial rule. Some 40 new states have emerged. White minorities rule South Africa and Rhodesia.

British rule of Egypt and Sudan established. Boer War ended. Chinese and Asians imported into South Africa. Moroccan crisis between Britain, France and Germany. Leopold II gave Congo to Belgian Government. Union of South Africa founded (1910). Ethiopian independence guaranteed. British conquered Northern Nigeria.

Egypt made a British protectorate, Morocco a French protectorate. Tripoli annexed by Italy. Botha Prime Minister of South Africa. 1914–18 War: German Togoland and Cameroons conquered. Botha took German South-West Africa. Prolonged campaign in East Africa. After the war, German colonies became mandates of Britain and France.

Moroccan leader Abd-el-Krim defeated Spanish, was beaten by French. Egypt an independent monarchy (1922), Britain kept military rights and Sudan. Kenya and Tanganyika set up. Southern Rhodesia given self-government. Term *apartheid* came into use in South Africa. Haile Selassie, Emperor of Ethiopia (1930).

Rise of nationalism in French Morocco. Italy claimed Tunisia. South Africa: National Government took office. Italian conquest of Ethiopia (1935–6). Egypt: accession of King Farouk, treaty with Britain. Italians invaded British Somaliland and Egypt in 1940; driven back by British.

Egypt under British military control. Ethiopia liberated. Italians, defeated in North Africa, were reinforced by German army under Rommel. Rommel defeated at Alamein (1942). French North Africa invaded by Anglo-American army. Axis troops driven out. South Africa at war with Germany and Japan, Nationalist Government (1948) began *apartheid* policy.

Sudan independent (1956). Mau-Mau rising in Kenya, Jomo Kenyatta imprisoned. Ghana independent (1957), Nkrumah Prime Minister. Many African states followed, including French Guinea, Chad, Niger, Madagascar, Nigeria and Ivory Coast. Rebellion in Algeria. Belgian Congo independent (1960); civil war.

Mobutu took control of Congo (1965). South Africa left Commonwealth. Sierra Leone, Tanganyika, Uganda, Kenya, Malawi, Zambia, Gambia etc. independent. Rhodesia declared U.D.I.; sanctions imposed. Verwoerd, South African premier, assassinated. Army coup in Nigeria, Biafran war. Nkrumah overthrown. Suez Canal closed.

The Americas

The U.S. achieved unparalleled wealth and power. Canada prospered while Latin America remained unstable.

Theodore Roosevelt President (1901); social reforms, big business controls, U.S. involvement in world affairs. Wright brothers flew. Model "T" Ford appeared. First cinemas. Canada: Alberta, Saskatchewan founded. Venezuela failed to pay European creditors. Writers: James, London, O. Henry. Music: birth of jazz and the blues.

Woodrow Wilson, President (1913); financial reforms. U.S. intervened in Mexico. Panama Canal opened (1914). War declared on Germany (1917). Wilson's 14 Points, advocacy of League of Nations rejected by Senate. First broadcasting stations set up. Canada: half a million men sent to war. Writers: Rice Burroughs. Cinema: Griffith.

Harding (1921) and Coolidge (1923) Presidents. Prohibition era. Immigration reduced. Lindbergh flew Atlantic. Hoover President (1929). Stock market crash. Latin America: trade expansion, co-operation with U.S. Mexico ruled by President Calles. Cinema: Chaplin. Music: Gershwin. Writers: Lewis, Hemingway, Fitzgerald.

The Depression. F. D. Roosevelt President (1933). New Deal measures to promote recovery. Prohibition ended. Social Security Act. Canada: Ottowa Economic Conference, 1932. Mexico: President Cardenas took over foreign oil properties. Bolivia and Paraguay at war. Writers: Caldwell, Steinbeck, Runyon, O'Hara. Cinema: Garbo, Gable, Marx Brothers.

U.S. at war with Germany and Japan. Truman, President (1945). San Francisco Conference. U.S. joined United Nations. Truman Doctrine. Marshall Aid. U.S. intervention in Korea. Canadian troops joined U.N. forces. Argentina: Peron dictator. industrialization. Chile: Communists active. Writers: Tennessee Williams, Miller, Thurber.

Truman dismissed MacArthur in Korea. Eisenhower President (1952). McCarthy anti-Communist campaign. H bomb exploded. Civil rights movement. Kruschev visited U.S. Cuba: Fidel Castro took over, hostility to U.S. Argentina: Peron overthrown. Latin American Free Trade Association formed. Music: birth of rock'n'roll. Cinema: Brando.

Kennedy President (1961). Space programme. Bay of Pigs invasion failed to oust Castro. Cuban crisis. Kennedy assassinated (1963); Johnson President. Anti-poverty programme. Widespread opposition to Vietnam war. Luther King assassinated. Race riots. Nixon President (1968). Moon landing (1969). Canada: Quebec separatism. Expo '67.

Index

CANADA*

BRITAIN*

UNITED STATES OF AMERICA

MAL

② Bermuda

BAHAMAS 1973

㉒

③ JAMAICA 1962

⑩

㉔

GAMBIA 1965

BARBADOS 1966

GRENADA 1974

TRINIDAD & TOBAGO 1962

SIERRA LEONE 1960

GHANA 1957

NIGE

**Dependencies,
colonies and
protectorates of U.K.,
Australia or New Zealand**

① Ascension I.
② Bermuda
③ British Honduras
④ British Solomon Is.
⑤ Cook I.
⑥ Falkland Is.
⑦ Gibraltar
⑧ Gilbert and Ellice Is.
⑨ Hong Kong
⑩ Leeward Is.
⑪ Macquairie Is.
⑫ New Britain
⑬ New Guinea
⑭ New Hebrides
⑮ New Ireland
⑯ Papua
⑰ Rhodesia
⑱ St Helena
⑲ Seychelles
⑳ South Georgia
㉑ South Sandwich
㉒ Turks and Caicos Is.
㉓ Tristan da Cunha
㉔ Windward Is.

GUYANA 1966

①

⑱

㉓

⑥

⑳

㉑

CYPRUS 1960

PAKISTAN 1947
(LEFT COMMONWEALTH 1972)

EAST PAKISTAN
(BANGLADESH FROM 1972)

INDIA 1947

⑨

CEYLON 1948
(NOW SRI LANKA)

MALAYSIA 1963

SINGAPORE 1961

⑧

DA 1962

KENYA 1963

⑲

⑮

NAURU 1968

IA 1964

⑫

⑬

⑧

MALAWI 1964

⑯

④

964

WESTERN SAMOA 1970

MAURITIUS 1968

⑭

⑤

NA 1966

FIJI 1970

SWAZILAND 1968

AUSTRALIA*

OTHO 1966

TONGA 1970

he Commonwealth and
he United States, circa 1970

NEW ZEALAND*

he Commonwealth, circa 1970   *Founder members   Dates refer to dates of accession

⑪